MEMOIRS OF THE
WAY HOME

MEMOIRS OF THE
WAY HOME

Ezra and Nehemiah as a Call to Conversion

Gerald M. Bilkes

Reformation Heritage Books
Grand Rapids, Michigan

Memoirs of the Way Home
© 2013 by Gerald M. Bilkes

Reformation Heritage Books
2965 Leonard St. NE
Grand Rapids, MI 49525
616-977-0889 / Fax 616-285-3246
orders@heritagebooks.org
www.heritagebooks.org

Printed in the United States of America
13 14 15 16 17 18/10 9 8 7 6 5 4 3 2 1

Library of Congress Cataloging-in-Publication Data

Bilkes, Gerald M.
  Memoirs of the way home : Ezra and Nehemiah as a call to conversion / by Gerald M. Bilkes.
     pages cm
  ISBN 978-1-60178-264-9 (pbk. : alk. paper) 1. Bible. Ezra—Textbooks. 2. Bible. Nehemiah—Textbooks. I. Title.
  BS1355.55.B55 2013
  222'.706—dc23
                              2013018132

For additional Reformed literature, request a free book list from Reformation Heritage Books at the above regular or e-mail address.

For my father and mother,
with love

Contents

Acknowledgments

This book is about a journey, but the publication itself has been a journey, with lots of thoughts of turning back! However, I am greatly indebted to Annette Gysen and Jay Collier of Reformation Heritage Books (RHB) for helping me along. I also want to thank David Woollin, Amy Zevenbergen, Linda den Hollander, and the other staff at RHB for seeing this book through to publication, and to Dr. Joel Beeke for agreeing to publish it. An initial draft of the chapters appeared in installments in the *Banner of Sovereign Grace Truth* and *The Messenger*, and I gratefully acknowledge the respective editors, Dr. Joel Beeke and Rev. Cornelis Pronk, for permission to publish them in this format.

A special thanks to my amazing wife, Michelle. How little I knew what an outstanding wife, mother, confidant, friend—and editor—I would marry! Thanks also to Kate DeVries and Pauline Timmer, my sister-in-law and mother-in-law, for their help in proofing the chapters at various points. Thanks to Ann Dykema for her faithful help with this and many other matters. I want to thank the students in Puritan Reformed Theological Seminary classes, who often helped improve my understanding of Ezra and Nehemiah. A special thank-you to Rev. Maarten Kuivenhoven and Dirk

Naves, my research assistants in the past, and Michael Borg, currently assisting me, for their work in the trenches. Any remaining errors are solely my own responsibility, though all of you have saved me from countless more.

Also, I appreciate the encouragement I've received from my seminary colleagues, Dr. Joel Beeke, Dr. David Murray, Dr. William VanDoodewaard, Dr. Michael Barrett, and Rev. Mark Kelderman. Working with you is a real privilege. I want to acknowledge the Free Reformed Churches, specifically the Theological Education Committee, for their oversight, help, and encouragement to publish this book. Finally, I wish to thank the Lord, who is both first and last!

In those days, and in that time, saith the LORD,
the children of Israel shall come, they and the children of Judah together,
going and weeping: they shall go, and seek the LORD their God.
They shall ask the way to Zion with their faces thitherward, saying,
Come, and let us join ourselves to the LORD
in a perpetual covenant that shall not be forgotten.

—JEREMIAH 50:4–5

INTRODUCTION

The year is 538 BC, and the Persian king, Cyrus, has just issued a proclamation that the Jewish exiles can return home. All throughout the Jewish settlements, the word spreads: "We can return home! We are free to go! The prophets were right. God has opened the prison doors of exile." For the next hundred years, waves of journeying groups travel the dusty roads from Babylon and Persia back to Judah. How would you like to be able to read some memoirs written by someone taking that journey?

We have not just one person's memoirs from this time, but two. Both Ezra and Nehemiah wrote down in first-person form what they saw, felt, and experienced as they left exile and came back to the Promised Land. No wonder the books of Ezra and Nehemiah have such an up-close and personal feel to them. Ezra was a scribe, living daily in the world of letters, words, and sentences, and handled the writings of Moses and the prophets preserved from former times. Nehemiah was a king's cupbearer, working in the world of royal influence and intrigue. Both of them put pen to paper to give us eyewitness accounts that involve anguish and adventure. And, best of all, it is inspired Scripture.

The Way Home

For the most part, the books of Ezra and Nehemiah are not the records of great heroic feats. They read more like the confessions of a humbled prodigal and bear an uncanny resemblance to the experiences of the younger son in Christ's parable of the prodigal son (Luke 15:11–32), traveling as he does from the far country back to the father's house. In many ways, the narratives in Ezra and Nehemiah read like an extended account of the prodigal's way back home. This journey has different phases, occurring over nearly a century. Yet through it all, it is foundationally a journey from misery to joy, from sadness to gladness, from captivity to service.

The Far Country of Exile

The exile had been punishment for a nation's sin, but it was more than that. When the nation of Israel (722 BC) and then the nation of Judah (587 BC) were led away into exile, the people were deported to the very countries whose idols they had worshiped. You could put it this way: As Israel pursued the idols of the nations, first their hearts journeyed into the far country. In exile, the rest of them followed. Early on, in their Father's house in Canaan, the people enjoyed life and communion with their God, especially during the days of Joshua and then later under David. But they repeatedly yearned after the gods of the surrounding nations and their way of life. Israel proved that it was bent on turning from the Lord's way. The people wasted their God-given gifts on false gods—idols that could be seen, handled, and manipulated. These idols promised happiness and success, though in the end they impoverished this pleasure-seeking nation and enslaved the people to cruel taskmasters.

Just as the prodigal son began to be in want (Luke 15:14–15), so, too, Israel found itself "in great distress" (Neh. 9:37), slaving away for others. As a nation, it had joined itself to strangers, and now it was at the mercy of foreign lords. In Nehemiah, we read this sad lament: "Behold, we are servants this day, and for the land that thou gavest unto our fathers to eat the fruit thereof and the good thereof, behold, we are servants in it" (9:36).

In Ezra and Nehemiah, we watch these prodigal people as they return home. In the deepest sense, this return wasn't about the actual march from Babylon to Judah, though that certainly gave concrete shape to it. The real journey home was much longer and far deeper. It was a profoundly spiritual journey. It involved confession of sin and separation from former loves. The process included steps forward and backward. But as is always the case in true conversion, the Father's drawing love prevailed over His people's wayward hearts.

A Century of Returning to the Land

Some debate exists as to the exact chronology of Ezra and Nehemiah. The following is the most commonly accepted chronology of the events in these books.

Historical Review (Ezra 1–6): In 538 BC, Cyrus allowed Jews to return to Judah and rebuild the temple. Those who did return took up the task of rebuilding. After some setbacks, the temple was finished in 515 BC.

Ezra's Memoirs (Ezra 7–10): In 458 BC, Ezra returned with a fresh wave of Jews to beautify the temple and teach the law of Moses in Jerusalem. He discovered a situation that was profoundly compromised and led the people in a national confession of sin.

Nehemiah's Memoirs (Nehemiah 1–13): In 445 BC, Nehemiah heard that the walls of Jerusalem were broken down. The king allowed him to return to rebuild them. When that work was completed, Ezra read the law to the people, and under the leadership of Ezra and Nehemiah, the people made a covenant with God. The book ends with great rejoicing (chapter 12), though Nehemiah later returned to make further reforms (chapter 13).

A Call to Us Today

When you examine these writings, you realize they are exceedingly relevant in light of the situation of many people today, especially those in the Western world. Essentially, these memoirs pose a challenge to us. Are we in the far country, or are we, by grace, on our way back home to God?

Like the prodigal, many of us once enjoyed innumerable spiritual privileges. We lived in the "Father's house" of biblical and evangelical truth. In general, however, the great Protestant churches of the Reformation have sold themselves into a new Babylonian captivity of sorts. The church of Christ has sold out to worldly thinking, material possessions, the pursuit of pleasure, and other idols. In most cases, we have not simply *lost* our heritage, but we have eagerly *left* our heritage.

Like Israel before its exile, we have cast a desiring look at the world around us. What we have seen has made us want to explore what the world has to offer. As a result, many prodigal sons of today have sold out to the "pig farmers" of our culture. At their mercy, we feed on the husks of entertainment, pleasure, and a worldly gospel. All the while, whether we realize it or not, our souls are more famished than ever.

"Turn Us, O God"

Even though the professing church of God finds itself, like Israel, in a sad and dilapidated condition, there are those today who, like Zerubbabel, Ezra, and Nehemiah, long to see it restored to its former glory. Psalm 102:14 describes people who "take pleasure in [Zion's] stones, and favour the dust thereof." They are elsewhere called "God's remnant." Isaiah says, "Except the LORD of hosts had left unto us a very small remnant, we should have been as Sodom, and we should have been like unto Gomorrah" (1:9). God has promised to leave such a remnant in every time. The Lord says in Zephaniah 3:12, "I will also leave in the midst of thee an afflicted and poor people, and they shall trust in the name of the LORD" (see 1 Kings 19:18; Rom. 11:4–5).

In times of spiritual decline, such people long for tokens of the Lord's mercy. They desire it just as people long for spring after a long, hard winter. They yearn for it like prisoners waiting for the day when they will be free again. These longings well up deep within believers' hearts and are breathed out in prayer. We read of these deep, heartfelt prayers in Scripture: "Turn again our captivity, O LORD, as the streams in the south" (Ps. 126:4). "Let the sighing of the prisoner come before thee; according to the greatness of thy power preserve thou those that are appointed to die" (Ps. 79:11). "Turn us again, O God of hosts, and cause thy face to shine; and we shall be saved" (Ps. 80:7). "Make us glad according to the days wherein thou hast afflicted us, and the years wherein we have seen evil" (Ps. 90:15). These are pleas for the Lord to return and have mercy on His church.

"Turn Ye to Me"

The Lord's call to His people today is exactly the same as it was to wayward Israel: "Turn ye unto me, saith the LORD of hosts, and I will turn unto you, saith the LORD of hosts" (Zech. 1:3). Nehemiah echoed this in his prayer to the Lord: "But if ye turn unto me, and keep my commandments, and do them; though there were of you cast out unto the uttermost part of the heaven, yet will I gather them from thence, and will bring them unto the place that I have chosen to set my name there" (1:9). And so it is God's call that effects the return of the people to Jerusalem and Judah in Ezra and Nehemiah. The call is reiterated in the opening verses of Ezra: "Who is there among you of all his people? his God be with him, and let him go up to Jerusalem, which is in Judah, and build the house of the LORD" (1:3).

While Cyrus actually is the one speaking these words, we need to see the Lord behind him, drawing the people back to Himself, and as the father in the parable of the prodigal son, gazing into the distance when the prodigal "was yet a great way off" (Luke 15:20). Have you ever wondered what motivated this younger son to return home? It was not only the desperate circumstances in which he found himself but also his father's loving heart. We read that when the son "came to himself," he thought about the things that his father's servants enjoyed (Luke 15:17). Under such a kind and compassionate master, these servants lived a good life. If his father was such a loving master, wasn't he worth returning to? And so this son's thoughts of his father's love drew him home.

So, too, God's love draws His people back to Him. It was not in Israel's power to turn to the Lord any more than it was in the prodigal's power to turn himself back to his father. Consider what the father says about his son after his return: "For this my son was dead, and is alive again; he was lost, and is found" (Luke 15:24). He refers to his son as dead! Something that is not living is not capable of action; by implication, then, the son would never have come back on his own. In Luke 15, Christ tells two other stories in connection with the prodigal son that underscore the point. A shepherd went looking for his lost sheep, and a woman swept and searched diligently for her lost coin. Neither a lost sheep nor a lost coin would find its way back to its owner by itself. And so the prodigal, too, was searched out and drawn home by a father's heart of love.

This corresponds well with the Bible's teaching about repentance. Nowhere in Scripture are we taught that we repent and return to God through the exercise of our free will. By our fall into sin, our wills have become enslaved to sin and the devil. We do not want to return to God. Jesus said to those who rejected Him: "And ye will not come to me, that ye might have life" (John 5:40). Without the work of God the Holy Spirit in their hearts, sinners will not turn to the Lord. They need the Lord to "give them repentance to the acknowledging of the truth; and that they may recover themselves out of the snare of the devil, who are taken captive by him at his will" (2 Tim. 2:25–26; see also Acts 5:31).

What are you to do when you find yourself in the "pigsty" of your own captivity? What are you to do when you find yourself tethered to the dictates of a godless culture, finding no real satisfaction in life? The answers to these questions are found in Ezra and Nehemiah. There we read the call, promise, and life of conversion in the memoirs of a prodigal people returning to their God.

Questions

1. What are some good reasons to keep a diary or write down some of the mercies of God in our lives?

2. Give some examples of prodigals in the Bible. How common is it to read of people returning from "far countries" back to the God who calls them?

3. Why do you think the books of Ezra and Nehemiah are in the Bible?

4. Why don't these books celebrate Ezra and Nehemiah? Whom do they celebrate?

5. Why should we cry to God to turn us?

~ 1 ~

THE LORD IS FIRST

Ezra 1:1–4

The first four verses of Ezra are so important that they are the focus of our entire first chapter. They show that everything good starts with God. The subject of the first sentence of Ezra is the Lord God. According to the first verse, "the LORD stirred up the spirit of Cyrus" to make a proclamation. In verse 5 (which we will cover in the next chapter), we will see how He also stirred the spirit of the people to return. The point clearly is this: God is first in the process of turning lost sinners back to Himself.

Advance Notice

A thousand years before the first chapter of Ezra, during the time of Moses, God told the people that He would be first in their restoration and repentance. Back in Deuteronomy, the Lord made very clear to the people of Israel how true repentance happens. He warned them that they would fall into idolatry, bringing on themselves punishment as a result. His servant Moses warned them where their prodigal hearts would take them: "The LORD shall scatter you among the nations, and ye shall be left few in number among the heathen, whither the LORD shall lead you. And there ye shall serve gods, the work of men's hands, wood and stone, which neither see, nor hear, nor eat, nor smell" (Deut. 4:27–28). This is precisely what happened. As a punishment for Israel's sins, the Lord did scatter them among the nations. However, Moses also told them: "When thou art in tribulation, and all these things are come upon thee, even in the latter days, if thou turn to the LORD thy God, and shalt be obedient unto his voice; (For the LORD thy God is a merciful God;) he will not forsake thee, neither destroy thee, nor forget the covenant of thy fathers which he sware unto them" (Deut. 4:30–31). In other words, almost a thousand years before it happened, the nation's repentance was foretold! Note these important words: "For the LORD thy God is a merciful God." God's mercy would bring the people to repentance and draw them back to Him. He would be the first to act; they would act in response.

What was true for Israel is also true for us. Behind every true conversion is the mercy of God. The Lord does not wait for us to initiate a return to Him—we take a few steps toward Him, and then He brings us the rest of the way. No, the Lord is "the first" (Isa. 44:6). His mercy is the only explanation for anyone's repentance. Let's see how this truth unfolds in the first four verses of the book of Ezra. Prodigal Israel will return home to its God only because He is acting powerfully, in accordance with His own promise.

He Speaks
In 538 BC, Cyrus, king of Persia, had defeated the Babylonian army and taken the city of Babylon. Before the rise of Persia,

Babylon, an old Assyrian province, was the sovereign power; this was the nation that had cast Judah into exile. Now Cyrus controlled the entire eastern part of the known world.

Impressive as Cyrus's accomplishments were, they are not the highlights of the book of Ezra. The author looks beyond this worldly king's work to the work of the Lord—the true and only Sovereign. According to the first verse of Ezra, "The LORD stirred up the spirit of Cyrus king of Persia" (emphasis added). Truly, "the king's heart is in the hand of the LORD" (Prov. 21:1). Cyrus may have thought he was directing affairs to his own advantage. Instead, the great King of heaven was directing the heart of Cyrus in order to fulfill His own purposes.

The sovereign Lord is a faithful Lord. He is faithful to His word. The book of Ezra makes this point at the outset: "that the word of the LORD...might be fulfilled" (v. 1). The Lord had spoken, promising through the prophet Jeremiah that the exile would last for only seventy years (Jer. 29:10). He had also promised that He would raise up Cyrus to bring His people home (Isa. 44:23–45:6). Now the Lord was acting to fulfill these promises.

Cyrus's official edict is recorded for us in verses 2–4. An edict is a royal proclamation announced by official messengers. It was probably carried to various cities of importance in order to reveal the king's will throughout his vast empire. Certainly, word must have reached the captive people of Israel. Perhaps they said to one another, "Did you hear the news? King Cyrus is allowing us to go back to our own land."

Certainly, this happy news should have melted their hearts. As they heard it, they had reason to remember that

God's word through His prophets Jeremiah and Isaiah was coming to fulfillment. What an amazing God the Lord was! They had deserved their captivity, for they had abandoned God. Though they had broken all their promises, the Lord was faithful to His word. Despite their faithlessness, God was proving Himself to be a faithful God and Redeemer.

He Acts

Notice the wording that Cyrus used in verse 2: "The LORD God of heaven hath given me all the kingdoms of the earth; and he hath charged me to build him an house at Jerusalem, which is in Judah." Cyrus's positive reference to the Lord does not mean that he knew Him in a saving relationship. He was not doing something entirely unique for the Jews here; historical records tell us that he took similar action on other occasions for other groups of people. Notice also that when Cyrus referred to God, he wrote: "*His* God be with him" (v. 3, emphasis added). Further on, the same verse literally says, "He is the God...*which is in Jerusalem*" (emphasis added). In both these instances Cyrus stopped short of calling God his God, and he did not see God as the only God of the world. Rather, he referred to God as the God of the Jews, limited in influence to the city of Jerusalem.

Nevertheless, although Cyrus did not have a personal faith in the Jews' God, he did at least openly and publicly acknowledge Him. How convicting this is to us who so often fail to acknowledge the Lord openly. We are so afraid of what people around us might think. But those who profess to be God's people should not be ashamed to acknowledge Him, even when the world around us finds it unpalatable. Perhaps it is part of the church's backslidden condition that we do not speak more openly and fearlessly about the Lord. Indeed, if we were to speak more openly of Him, we might be exposed to subtle or even overt persecution. But we would also enjoy more of a sense of the Lord's favor if we feared Him more than we fear the people around us (Acts 4:29–31).

Many people today, like Cyrus, will allow for the God of the Bible to be *a* God, but not the *only* God. People sometimes speak of the "Christian" God, as if there are many gods and many ways to heaven. We live in what some call postmodern times, in which people think we need to tolerate all kinds of worldviews, even if they contradict each other. We should resist being a part of this postmodern chorus, even if we think it may serve us well in this world. As people who have been freed by God, we ought to unashamedly take our direction from God's Word, which says, "Say among the heathen that the LORD reigneth" (Ps. 96:10).

Still today, the faithful Lord is overturning kingdoms and establishing governments, all in accordance with His will (Dan. 2:21). As we see God's work in our day, we should remember Christ's words: "And when these things begin to come to pass, then look up, and lift up your heads; for your redemption draweth nigh" (Luke 21:28). God Himself is in all the events of our time. He is acting to bring all things to their culmination—the redemption of His people and the full ushering in of His kingdom.

He Calls

The king's edict called the Lord's people to identify themselves: "Who is there among you of all his people?" (v. 3).

Imagine Cyrus's messenger reading this edict in public squares or posting it on city gates throughout the region. Imagine the word spreading: "Can you believe it? The king is looking for the people who call themselves by the name of the LORD!" For a moment, King Cyrus acted as the Lord's mouthpiece, calling His exiled people home.

It's important to remember from what circumstances God's people were being called home. Their captivity hadn't just come upon them through some unfortunate political situation. This was the punishment they had brought on themselves. It was God's covenantal discipline as a result of their sin—the curses of the law and the judgments of the prophets had come upon them. Remember, these events had been foretold! And so, in a way, we could say these people had chosen exile, like the prodigal in Christ's parable. Their wayward hearts had become infatuated with the idols of the surrounding nations. How fitting a punishment their exile really was! By going after heathen gods, they brought themselves exile in a heathen land—and no gods could deliver them from that. Only their God could.

Some of these captives surely understood this. For instance, Daniel's prayer shows that he was conscious of the cause of the people's punishment—namely, sin. He confessed:

> Neither have we obeyed the voice of the LORD our God, to walk in his laws, which he set before us by his servants the prophets. Yea, all Israel have transgressed thy law, even by departing, that they might not obey thy voice; therefore the curse is poured upon us, and the oath that is written in the law of Moses the servant of God, because we have sinned against him (9:10–11).

Another example is Nehemiah, who acknowledged:

> We have dealt very corruptly against thee, and have not
> kept the commandments, nor the statutes, nor the judg-
> ments, which thou commandedst thy servant Moses.
> Remember, I beseech thee, the word that thou com-
> mandedst thy servant Moses, saying, If ye transgress, I
> will scatter you abroad among the nations: but if ye turn
> unto me, and keep my commandments, and do them;
> though there were of you cast out unto the uttermost
> part of the heaven, yet will I gather them from thence,
> and will bring them unto the place that I have chosen to
> set my name there (1:7–9).

People who shared Daniel's and Nehemiah's repentant
spirit would have much cause for thanksgiving because of
Cyrus's edict. God's faithfulness was so evident in this good
news! Here was a way of escape from the punishment they
had brought on themselves. What a covenant-keeping God
was theirs!

Other Jews, however, saw things differently. They had
enjoyed blending into the heathen culture around them.
They didn't see their new life in Babylon as bondage. They
felt no inclination to answer Cyrus's call: "Who is there
among you of all his people?" (v. 3). Something held them
back, even though many of their fellow Jews were packing
their few belongings in preparation for the trip home.

Isn't this how many people today respond to the gospel
call? They may hear that they are sinners in bondage who
need repentance. They may hear the gracious gospel promises of God. But, at the end of the day, they go on living as
they have always lived. They do not respond to God's call

because they can still make ends meet on their own. The love of a covenant-keeping God has not conquered their hearts, so they remain willingly in the bondage of sin and death.

He Draws

God was using Cyrus to draw these prodigal people home. Cyrus's pronouncement included the amazing phrase "his God be with him" (v. 3). For a prodigal people who return to the Lord, it is a miracle that God is their God and that He is with them. They know they don't deserve it, but there is always some "apprehension of God's mercy" in true repentance, as the Westminster Larger Catechism says so well:

> Repentance unto life is a saving grace, wrought in the heart of a sinner by the Spirit and Word of God, whereby, out of the sight and sense, not only of the danger, but also of the filthiness and odiousness of his sins, and upon the *apprehension of God's mercy* in Christ to such as are penitent, he so grieves for and hates his sins, as that he turns from them all to God, purposing and endeavoring constantly to walk with him in all the ways of new obedience (emphasis added).

Notice the next part of Cyrus's pronouncement: "His God be with him, and let him *go up*" (v. 3, emphasis added). The Hebrew verb here is specific; in contrast to other verbs that might signify going down or going straight, this word means going up and was often used to describe going to worship. In other words, Cyrus was suggesting that there was something sacred about this journey home. The exile had been a low point in the Jews' history, but now God was drawing His people up from the depths of their captivity.

He Employs

The land of Judah, the city of Jerusalem, and the temple were in complete ruins. Their stones were thrown down and ground to dust. The land lay in a winter of desolation. But the returning prodigals loved these ruined stones; they felt drawn to the dust (see Ps. 102:14). Seeing the Lord's house in such a state, they were motivated to rebuild it in the hope that it would achieve its former glory. They would rather spend one day in the ruined courts of the Lord than a thousand in Babylon. Attending to the Lord's house and service was their delight because it meant being with the God of the universe. In calling His people back, God was turning captives into builders. Even now, Cyrus's edict made provision for them—with silver, gold, goods, beasts, and freewill offerings (v. 4). This, too, was a confirmation of God's word. As Isaiah had prophesied, "Ye shall eat the riches of the Gentiles, and in their glory shall ye boast yourselves" (61:6; see also 60:15–17).

And so it is today. Whenever God works in His grace, He takes those in captivity to sin and frees them by Christ's Spirit. He brings them back to His house, and He provides for their every need. His promises are all fulfilled. Truly, He is both first and last!

Questions

1. Read the Lord's promise in Isaiah 44:24–28. How was He fulfilling this promise in Ezra 1?

2. We are often surprised when the Lord does what He has promised. What does that say about us?

3. Why is there no true repentance without a sense of God's mercy?

4. The Bible speaks of Cyrus as the Lord's servant. We know that Christ was the ultimate and perfect Servant of the Lord. He also proclaimed an edict to His people after He had won the greatest victory, and we find it in Matthew 28:18–20. What similarities and differences are there between Cyrus's and Christ's edicts?

5. In Ezra 1, Cyrus acknowledged that the Lord had given him all the kingdoms of the earth (v. 2). Compare this with Revelation 11:15. How should we understand this? What implications should this have for our view of this world?

6. To start a journey back to Jerusalem in Ezra's time would not have been easy. A traveler then would have to dare to be different and could also expect many dangers. How do these realities carry over into the journey of a life of repentance?

AWAKENING MERCY

Ezra 1:5–2:70

The Bible compares the life of unconverted sinners to a state of sleep. Of course, the wicked aren't literally sleeping their lives away. Figuratively speaking, though, they are living in a dreamland. Imagine a prisoner who falls asleep in his jail cell and begins to dream. In his dream, he is free again. Perhaps he imagines he is a wealthy and prestigious man who is able to do anything he wants. But when the prisoner awakes from his dream, he realizes his freedom, wealth, and prestige were only figments of his imagination. So, too, the wicked will one day wake up and realize that everything they were and thought have amounted to nothing of value. They will realize what they really were—captives of sin and death. No wonder that Paul writes to the Ephesians: "Awake thou that sleepest, and arise from the dead, and Christ shall give thee life" (5:14).

What happens, then, in conversion can be compared to awakening from sleep. Whether you experience it over a shorter or longer period of time, conversion is a waking up to the realities of life and death. Things you once thought were true now appear to be a sham, while other realities you never reckoned with are now undeniable. Christ described this awakening in His parable of the prodigal son, as He spoke of the young man coming to himself, or coming to his senses (Luke 15:17). Before that time, he had been living in a sort of dreamland, thinking he could do what he wanted to do and be what he wanted to be. He was the center of his own universe! But this was only a dream, and he needed to wake up to reality.

We want to take a closer look at the events of Ezra 1:5–2:70. Why did the people in this passage return from exile? Ezra 1:5 gives us the ultimate reason for their return. It refers to "all them whose spirit God had raised." The original Hebrew word, which is translated "raised" in this verse, literally means that God "awakened" or "roused" these people. And so, as Ezra 2:64 tells us, a congregation of 42,360 "awakened" people journeyed toward Jerusalem.

The fact that God roused these people implies, of course, that they needed to be awakened. They were in some sort of spiritual slumber. The apostle Paul explicitly warns us against spiritual drowsiness in 1 Thessalonians 5:6: "Therefore let us not sleep, as do others; but let us watch and be sober." If we are not awake, we are oblivious to the reality around us, and we are not attuned to God, His Word, His calls, or the spiritual dangers that surround us.

When God converts us, however, He wakes us up to many things. In a certain sense, the whole of the Christian life is discovering reality more and more. We discover who we are to a deeper extent. We discover who the Lord is to a greater degree. We come to see the world more and more in the light of God's Word. This doesn't always happen at a steady pace, though. Often God's people go through times of drowsiness again, and, at some level, they continue to need awakening grace. Sometimes they may feel so "asleep" that they might even wonder if they have ever truly been awakened to new life. Let's look at four specific marks that characterize a heart that has been awakened by God's grace.

Awakened to Hear

The first mark of those whom God awakens through salvation is that they hear in such a way that they heed God's Word. We saw in the previous chapter that God used Cyrus's edict to call His people out of their exile. Now we see what effect this call has. The hearts of some of the Jews were stirred to hear and heed this call. Through Cyrus, God had said, "Go up" (1:3). And now we read of those who "rose up" (1:5). Not everyone heeded the call. Countless people must have heard it but never heeded it. In fact, verse 5 mentions only people from "Judah and Benjamin" heeding the call, while we have no record of the response of the other ten tribes, many of whom were also scattered throughout these areas. This is the first evidence of awakening grace: we hear God's call so as to heed it in His strength.

Awakened to Depart

A second mark of God's awakening work is that we begin a journey following God's call. Ezra 2:1 gives us a rather succinct account of the journey home: "Now these are the children of the province that went up out of the captivity… and came again unto Jerusalem and Judah, every one unto his city." This journey back to Jerusalem would have been a difficult one. However, like Christian in *Pilgrim's Progress*, these people felt compelled to leave their homes and travel to the place where God was calling them. As they made the journey, God surrounded them with evidences of His care. One of the most important things provided for them was a group of leaders (see 1:5; 2:2). One of the leaders is specifically mentioned in 1:8: "Sheshbazzar, the prince of Judah." Some have wondered whether this man was a descendant of King David, but we don't know for sure. We do know that as a prince of Judah, he had the unique opportunity of leading the people on their first return to Jerusalem, taking with him the treasures of God's house. King Nebuchadnezzar had taken these treasures at the time of the captivity, but Cyrus returned them (1:7). These treasures would have included firepans, pots, shovels, and other items used in the temple (see 2 Kings 25:13–17). Now they could again be used for their proper purpose in the service of God.

Just as the Hebrews had left Egypt with much spoil (Ex. 11:2), so, too, the remnant of Jews left Babylon with great treasures. God made the surrounding people willing to strengthen the hands of His returning people, and they gave the Jews vessels of silver and gold, goods, beasts, and precious things. The sheep of the Good Shepherd were provided with everything they needed!

Awakened to Belong

The third mark of those whom God awakens through salvation is that they are gathered with the people of God. They know themselves united with other true children of God and love them and desire to be reckoned among them. This is how we should understand the attention given to names in Ezra 2, a list that is repeated with slight differences in Nehemiah 7. These chapters record the numbers of the people who returned from Babylon to Judah in a first wave. They returned under twelve leaders, as Nehemiah 7:7 makes clear. The list is a very orderly one. In Ezra 2, people were registered by clans (vv. 3–20), cities and towns (vv. 21–35), or specific temple functions (vv. 36–58). Special attention is given to the temple workers. Among them were priests, Levites, singers, porters, Nethinim, and the children of Solomon's servants. We don't know a lot about the last two of these groups. According to Ezra 8:20, the Nethinim (literally, "given" or "dedicated" ones) assisted the Levites, probably with the more mundane tasks in the temple. The children of Solomon's servants were probably another specialized group of laborers at the temple (see 1 Kings 5:6, 15).

This long list serves a threefold purpose. First, it shows how important it was to the returning Jews to be the Lord's people (see 2:62). This was the core of their identity! They wanted to be registered as the people of God. Chapter 2:2 speaks of "the men of the people of Israel," and the Israelites, of course, were God's chosen people. Isaiah had prophesied of this desire to be the Lord's people: "One shall say, I am the LORD's; and another shall call himself by the name of Jacob; and another shall subscribe with his hand unto the LORD, and surname himself by the name of Israel" (44:5).

Second, the list demonstrates that God is pleased to work through families, in the line of the generations. Many of those in exile would now return to take their forefathers' inheritance, continuing the family name in the Land of Promise. Notice that the word "children" is the most frequently recurring word in the list. Clearly, not every child of the named men returned, but many did. What a blessing it is when God works along generational lines! Although we can't presume upon it, we ought to plead fervently for grace for our children, that they might truly belong to the Lord by a Spirit-worked faith.

Third, the list highlights the importance of the returning Jews' genealogical credentials. Mention is made of those in the group who were not able to show proof of their family lineage (2:59–63). In fact, even some of the priests "could not show…whether they were of Israel" (2:59). Perhaps these people's parents had been negligent in entering them into the national registry. It is even possible that some of them were imposters who were hoping to stake a claim to land by pretending to be part of the Jewish nation. For whatever reason, these people's identity could not be proven. And so they were not able to claim land or take up their priestly office like the others did and needed to wait until the congregation could consult the will of the Lord.

Today, we no longer use genealogies in the same way. But how important it is that our names are written in the Lamb's Book of Life! The membership records of our churches may be inaccurate in some detail, but this Book of Life is perfect and accurate. What a mercy that Christ has come! He was made a priest "not after the law of a carnal commandment, but after the power of an endless life" (Heb. 7:16), which means that He became a priest not because He belonged to a line of human descent but because God the Father granted Him the resurrection from the dead. He is "a priest for ever after the order of Melchizedek" (Ps. 110:4).

Awakened to Worship

The final mark that God had awakened these people was their fear and worship of Him. Ezra 2 is not simply the registry of a nation. It is a registry of a nation of priests! The overall picture we get from the chapter is that of a nation of returning prodigals who were dedicated to and participating in the building up of God's temple. Each of them was involved, in some way, in the worship of God. Notice how verses 36–58 focus on the temple tasks. We already saw how the people brought back the temple implements for the worship of God. As chapter 2 ends, we note the reference to the chief of the fathers offering "freely for the house of God to set it up in his place" (v. 68). These were not simply immigrants seeking a better life. Everything focuses ultimately on the worship or glory of God.

Human beings have been created for the worship of God. Left to ourselves, we will never accomplish this because we continually suppress the truth in unrighteousness and worship the creation rather than the Creator (Rom. 1:18–32).

There is hope, however, for captives to sin and Satan in the Lord Jesus Christ. He never needed to be awakened from spiritual slumber. He was always going about His Father's business. He could truly say, "I have glorified thee on the earth" (John 17:4). Now, only through Him can people offer "freely for the house of God." When Christ took the sins of His people to Himself, we could say that God excluded Him from His register so that sinners like us might, for His sake, be registered as His people. On the basis of Christ's sacrifice for sin, God still today awakens sinners who come short of His glory. He awakens them to heed His call, to leave the city of destruction and belong to the people of God, and to begin through the Spirit to "present [their] bodies a living sacrifice, holy, acceptable unto God" (Rom. 12:1).

Questions

1. How did God raise people from their spiritual drowsiness in Ezra's day? How does He do it now? Review the marks that show if a person has been awakened.

2. The Lord made sure that these awakened people did not have to fend for themselves. What does this show us about how the Lord works when He awakens sinners today?

3. It is remarkable that God supplied twelve leaders for this early stage of the return (2:2; Neh. 7:7). What useful purposes can leaders in the church serve today?

4. Reflect on some of the differences between the registry in Ezra 2 and the Lamb's Book of Life (Rev. 21:27).

5. According to Ezra 2:61–63, some priests were barred from the priesthood because their names could not be found on the priestly registry. Why was Christ able to serve as the most perfect High Priest even though He did not descend from a priestly line? How does Hebrews 7:16 explain this?

6. True awakening calls people to worship, but it also impacts their worship. How will worship be different once awakening has occurred?

~ 3 ~

TOKENS OF MERCY

Ezra 3

The first step the prodigal took toward his father's house may have been a small one, but behind it was an entire change of heart. We are often tempted to consider small changes in our own or others' lives to be insignificant, but the Bible warns against that attitude (see Zech. 4:10). Even if they seem small, God's actions are always great. Their origin is in eternity past, where God decreed all His works. And they will last into eternity future, serving the glory of God's worthy name.

It is remarkable that Ezra 3 does not give much attention to the people's arrival in the land of Israel. We might have expected a detailed description of how the people crossed the boundary into their old homeland, how they went about locating their ancestral lands, or how they built temporary housing for themselves. Instead, the focus is on other things, and we will look at four of them, which were tokens of mercy and harbingers of good things to come.

Appointed Mediators

First, the Lord raised up appointed and consecrated leaders for these returning people. We read that Joshua and

Zerubbabel "stood up" with their associates (v. 2). Joshua was a priest, and Zerubbabel, one of King David's descendants, was governor. They were the "two anointed ones" who stood by the Lord of the whole earth (see Zech. 4:14). Like David, they were devoted to "find out a place for the LORD, an habitation for the mighty God of Jacob" (Ps. 132:5). The cooperation between these two men evidences the unique bond that existed between the priestly and kingly offices of Israel. Remember, Israel was a *kingdom of priests.* Both offices were needed for the reestablishment of the Jews as a holy people. And so God used Joshua and Zerubbabel to inspire His people to action, building His house.

What a mercy it is to have someone whom God has anointed standing between you and Him, especially if that one is able to help set up an altar that symbolizes acceptance with God. What was here represented by these two men, Joshua and Zerubbabel, would, in the fullness of time, need to be only one—namely, Jesus Christ, whom we could call "a royal priest" (see Ps. 110:1, 4).

A Bloody Altar

The Lord's second token of mercy was His provision of an altar of blood for the people (vv. 2–3). The people had come home to a land without a temple and, therefore, without a way of access to God. Joshua and Zerubbabel must have recognized this, for, in verse 2, we see them make the building of the altar their first priority. The altar needed to be built before the Holy of Holies, the golden candlesticks, or anything else in the temple. Having just returned from the exile because of sin, the people had to deal with their guilt first. They needed the blood of cleansing (see Zech. 3:1–4).

This altar was built according to God's design, as prescribed long ago by Moses (v. 2). This means that the Jews would have constructed a square altar of wood with horns in the four corners and overlaid with brass (see Ex. 27:1–8; 38:1–8). They took care to follow these specifications, for this was God's prescription for sinners who wanted to approach Him.

Because they feared the surrounding people, the priests had the altar inaugurated before the rest of the temple was completed (v. 3). Their concern is understandable. The altar was a visual display of God's grace and forgiveness; it would be a central element in their worship. They couldn't do without it! It was best to inaugurate it before the people around them attacked or interfered with their work in some other way. Their fears would later prove warranted, as we will see in Ezra 4. For now, though, the Jews had their altar, to which the surrounding people had no rights.

What an experience it must have been to see the way of access to the Lord rebuilt after decades of ruin and neglect! The burnt offerings on this altar would speak of atonement, forgiveness, and the return of God's favor (Lev. 1:4, 13, 17). So, too, what a spiritual blessing it is when God gives sight of the altar that Christ Jesus is for His people (see Heb. 13:10). That blessing is far greater than a mere token of mercy. It is a glorious abundance of mercy!

A Sure Foundation

A third token of the Lord's mercy was His provision for building the temple's foundation. Though the altar had been completed, God did not yet have a dwelling place among His people (v. 6). The work needed to be "set forward" (v. 8). God Himself would make this happen!

Notice again that Joshua and Zerubbabel, God's anointed ones, would provide leadership. All those who come out of the captivity, from twenty years old on up, would be involved in the building project (v. 8). They would act "as one man" with a single purpose (v. 1). These words in verse 1 remind us of Psalm 133, where we read of brothers dwelling in unity (v. 1). The psalm pictures this as oil running from the head of the priest down the whole body, all the way to the hem of the garment, consecrating the entire body to the Lord's service (v. 2). Can you picture the scene here as Joshua and Zerubbabel, the anointed ones, lead the way? It's as if the "oil of anointing" flowed down from the head (Joshua and Zerubbabel) all the way to the hem of the garment (the workers). There was brotherly unity among them.

In response to this token of mercy, the priests and Levites did exactly what we would expect: they blessed God. In full ceremonial dress, the priests marked the occasion with trumpet blasts and the Levites with cymbals in praise to the mercy of the Lord. Notice the words of their song: "He is good, for his mercy endureth for ever toward Israel" (v. 11). The people credited the progress to God's faithfulness. They could have echoed Psalm 126:3: "The LORD hath done great things for us; whereof we are glad."

This foundation points to the Lord Jesus Christ, whom Paul calls the only foundation of the church (1 Cor. 3:11). This foundation was proof that God has seen fit to dwell with sinners—to be present among His people—despite all their sin and unfaithfulness. If your life has been built on this only foundation, do you not have reason humbly to praise Him for His mercy?

Mixed Emotions

We will see in Ezra 4 that while the Jews rejoiced at the tokens of mercy and goodness the Lord had given them, the surrounding people did not share in their joy. They thought of the work as a needless, exclusive, and offensive undertaking.

It is also important to notice that even the Jews' joy was not unbounded. Verse 13 leaves us with a picture of joy mixed with sorrow, shouting with weeping. Those who were far away heard only a loud noise, but those who were close enough to the crowd saw that this was more than just shouting for joy. The older ones wept sorrowfully as they remembered the temple of Solomon in the days before its ruin. They knew that something had been lost that could never be recovered. The new temple would never be as glorious as the first one had been. How understandable that their emotions were mixed at this moment.

Returning prodigals can still identify with this mixture of emotions today (see Rom. 7:24–25; 1 Cor. 7:30). The apostle Paul notes the paradox of the Christian life: "As sorrowful, yet always rejoicing" (2 Cor. 6:10). What reason we have for sorrow when we look at our sins and shortcomings! Yet what reason we have for joy when we look at what our Savior has done for us! The Lord's people are waiting for the day when there will be no more sadness—when all tears will be wiped away (Rev. 7:17).

From a certain perspective, the events of Ezra 3 could be called small and unimpressive. But awakened sinners learn not to despise the day of small things (Zech. 4:10). They learn to see mercy woven through the slightest thing God gives them. Though their joy now is not as full as it will one day be, every token of mercy is cause to acknowledge the Lord.

Questions

1. What other things do we learn about Joshua (also called Jeshua) and Zerubbabel when we compare Haggai 1–2; Zechariah 3–4; and Matthew 1:12–13?

2. What similarities and differences are there between the building project in this chapter and what Christ does when He builds His spiritual temple (Eph. 2:18–22; 1 Peter 2:4–10)?

3. We are told that these people acted as "one man" (v. 1). Scripture teaches that there is a spiritual unity to the people of God in Christ (see Eph. 4:4). How do we see this in evidence today, and what do divisions do to this?

4. What attributes of the Lord did the people focus on in their praise? (See v. 11.) Why do you think they highlighted these attributes?

5. What different emotions does this chapter mention, and what can you say about the place these emotions have in spiritual life today?

6. When a returning prodigal looks to the blood of Christ for pardon and rests on Christ as the only foundation for time and eternity, few in the world take notice. What do the people in Ezra 3 teach us to do with such small things?

~ 4 ~

ADVERSARIES, SUBTLE AND SEVERE

Ezra 4

Nothing stirs up more resistance than a sinner's turning back to God. After Paul, the persecutor of Christ, fell on his face before the ascended Christ, his former collaborators "watched the gates day and night to kill him" (Acts 9:24). After all, the adversary of God sees repentance as desertion. Until we truly repent, we are "safely" in the camp of the enemy, blind to the fact that we are doing his bidding. We think we are our own lords and masters, but, as the Bible says, we are in "the snare of the devil," "taken captive by him at his will" (2 Tim. 2:26). No wonder he is enraged when a soul is snatched from his control! One step in true repentance unleashes the fury of hell. Let's look more closely at this chapter, in which God's people meet with resistance as their adversaries arrive on the scene.

Wolves in Sheep's Clothing
The adversaries of the Jews in chapter 4 were descendants of the people whom the Assyrian rulers had brought from the eastern provinces of their empire. These newcomers had intermingled and intermarried with some of the people

who stayed behind when the northern tribes of Israel were carried away captive (2 Kings 17), forming the mixed population that would eventually be called the Samaritans during the New Testament era. These people had manipulated the truths of God's Word to accommodate their religious views; thus, at the deepest level, there was an irreconcilable difference between the Jews and them.

These adversaries did not immediately launch an all-out attack in an effort to stop the Jews' work. Their first tactic was to encourage ecumenism. "Ecumenism," as we are using it here, refers to unifying different groups at the expense of truth. They did this by asking the Jews if they could join in building the temple. They were essentially saying, "We have Jewish blood in us too! We're worshiping the same Lord, even if we worship in different ways. Because there is no big difference between us and you, we want to join you and help with this building project."

On the surface, this proposal seemed attractive. They were offering to join forces and help shoulder the burden. Not only did they claim to have the same God, but they also wanted to unite in worshiping Him. A group of returning exiles could certainly use such friends! It seemed too good to be true. You can imagine some of the Jews' reasoning: "We won't have to give up anything. They won't force any changes on us. They aren't even asking for any payment or exchange of services. They just want to help!" Indeed, it was a tempting proposal. If they accepted it, the Jews would seemingly gain so much. If they rejected it, they would remain a small, outnumbered group of people.

But this was the bait that hid the trap. With God-given insight, Zerubbabel and Joshua saw the trap and unmasked the ploy. They replied, "Ye have nothing to do with us to build an house unto our God" (v. 3). Although this response may seem a harsh and unloving one, it shows that the true fear of God had called the returning exiles to be a holy nation, a peculiar people, specifically registered as the *Lord's* people (Deut. 14:2). They were not to be like the nations around them or to join with them.

This did not mean, of course, that the Jews would not have welcomed true converts to the worship of God. But it does mean that, short of true faith in their God, there was no basis for unity between the Jews and the surrounding nations. Cooperating with these Samaritans would make the Jews guilty of what Paul warned against later—yoking unequally with unbelievers (see 2 Cor. 6:14).

Voices like the Samaritans' are everywhere in Christendom today. Many call for a unity that would rob the truth of the gospel from the people of God. For example, some believe that Christians can have interfaith services with Jews or Muslims. Others believe that Reformed and Roman Catholic churches share the same essential doctrines about salvation. Ecumenism, with its emphasis on unity and strength in numbers, can be a real temptation, especially for younger people. Many today in institutions of higher learning are skilled at erasing or hiding important distinctions and painting the vision of a unified utopia. But a unified utopia is a mirage.

We need the insight and courage of Joshua and Zerubbabel to remain separate when God's Word demands it. We need the wisdom of Christ, who was tempted in all the same points as His people yet did not sin (Heb. 4:15). When He was tempted to bow down to Satan, Christ replied decisively: "Thou shalt worship the Lord thy God, and him only shalt thou serve" (Matt. 4:10). May God give us the same steadfastness!

Let's be on our guard against "wolves," who still seek to devour the church of God today. Many approach the church with olive branches. They seek to be united under the common cause of the church while they herald toleration among differing worldviews. But the professing people of God must stand fast with her Lord, even if they are the object of ridicule and intolerance.

Wolves without Sheep's Clothing

When opposed by God's people, some of these "uniters" become the most vicious attackers. So, too, when these Samaritans were refused, they promptly shed their niceties. They did not bother to appear as angels of light anymore; instead, they showed their true colors and began opposing the Jews openly. No longer were they wolves in sheep's clothing. They were just plain wolves.

The enemies began waging both spiritual and psychological warfare against God's people. According to verses 4–5, they had three powerful weapons: discouragement, fear, and political pressure. First, they used the weapon of *discouragement*. This is what the phrase "weakened the hands" means. They understood how debilitating discouragement can be, and they assailed the small group with it. Their hope was that the Jews would lose their confidence and focus, becoming weak in the process.

Second, the adversaries used the weapon of *fear*. The word "troubled" in verse 4 suggests that they sought to terrify the Jews, or make them anxious. Fear is such a difficult thing to combat! It can render us frozen. These enemies' strategy against the Jews was similar to that of Rabshakeh, the general of the Assyrian army, who used the weapon of fear at the time of the Jerusalem siege during the days of Hezekiah. From outside the city walls, Rabshakeh taunted the people in their own language, trying to make them afraid (see 2 Kings 18:19–25). When we are tempted to fear in this way, we should remember David's resolve: "What time I am afraid, I will trust in thee" (Ps. 56:3). David also encourages us with these words: "The LORD is my light and my salvation; whom shall I fear? the LORD is the strength of my life; of whom shall I be afraid?" (Ps. 27:1).

Third, the adversaries used *political pressure*. They hired (or bribed) advisers to "frustrate their purpose" through political means (v. 5). Their goal was nothing less than completely ending the Jews' building activity. Just as Balak hired Balaam to curse Israel, these enemies used hired counselors against the Jews "all the days of Cyrus" (v. 5). Their animosity continued into the reign of Ahasuerus (v. 6). We are told that the enemies wrote a letter to Ahasuerus (referred to also as Artaxerxes) to accuse the Jews (v. 6). It is probably this letter that is spelled out for us in verses 11–16; in it the enemies refer to "the rebellious and the bad city" (v. 12). What thinly veiled hatred is evident in their writing!

Their letter achieved its desired goal. We read words from the king's response that must have occasioned much grief and sorrow among the Jews: "Give ye now commandment to cause these men to cease, and that this city be not builded" (v. 21). Everything had to come to a grinding halt. The construction site became a forlorn place of unfinished work and a monument, you might say, of dashed dreams and unfulfilled desires.

The enemy of God loves to use political pressures against the cause of Christ. In the book of Acts, we also see political pressure being used against God's people. For example, think of when Paul and Silas were dragged before the rulers at Philippi (Acts 16:19). However, as the Bible also proves repeatedly, God controls all things, even the hearts of the rulers of this world. It may look as though human governments are able to frustrate God's cause, but in reality, the Lord's ultimate cause is only furthered, which Paul observes in Philippians 1:12: "But I would ye should understand, brethren, that the things which happened unto me have fallen out rather unto the furtherance of the gospel."

The Bible makes clear that the world always speaks against God's church (Acts 28:22). Happily, the Word of God speaks differently: "Glorious things are spoken of thee, O city of God" (Ps. 87:3). Christians must be prepared for a long, drawn-out battle with their enemy. There is no quick "exit strategy" in this battle. Only after God's people have crossed the Jordan will the Lord Himself unbuckle their armor and exchange it for victory robes and palm branches.

Who Will Have the Last Word?

The events of this chapter may seem discouraging developments to us. What temptations, trials, and hostility these Jews had to face! However, at a deeper level, this chapter is actually an encouragement for those who have begun the journey back to God. Despite dangers and difficulties they experience, these Jews should remind us of God's guiding hand over His people. It is He who gives them wisdom in temptation and helps them persevere through many trials.

We ought to be thankful that the Bible is such an honest book. So many times, we can relate to those in Scripture who face temptations and experience defeat. Many of us might be able to relate to the sad note on which this chapter seems to end: "Then ceased the work" (v. 24). There are times in our lives as believers when it seems as though we can't do anything more, as if the enemy has finally gotten the victory over us.

But notice that verse 24 goes on to say, "So it ceased *unto* the second year of the reign of Darius king of Persia" (emphasis added). The Jews' enemies will not have the last word! Neither will the enemies of any true believer. Christ will be the final victor. He said of another temple—the temple of His body: "Destroy this temple, and in three days I will raise it up" (John 2:19). The gates of hell cannot prevail against His church.

Questions

1. Read Ezra 4:1 again. What message must the building of a temple to the Lord have sent to these neighboring nations? What was so threatening about it?

2. Scripture tells us openly that these people were "adversaries" (v. 1). The Word of God is very open and honest about adversaries of God and His cause.

How is that helpful to us? How can we distinguish between friends and adversaries?

3. Read Ezra 4:3 and John 4:22. What light do Jesus' words shed on Ezra 4:3? What further light does John 4:23–24 shed on how to worship the Lord truly today?

4. Why might God have allowed these returning people to face such subtlety and hostility so early on? What kind of purpose does He have in allowing His people to interface with such enemies?

5. The enemies called the city of Jerusalem "rebellious" and "bad" (v. 12). What are some of the ways the church receives a bad name today?

6. At the end of the chapter, we see hands hanging down. What encouragement does Isaiah 35:3–4 offer returning prodigals for this condition?

~ 5 ~

FRESH COURAGE THROUGH THE WORD

Ezra 5

Those whom God has graciously converted are called the meek of the earth (Matt. 5:5). Their spiritual pride has been dealt a fundamental blow, and they have received the gospel in meekness, realizing that God's grace is undeserved. This spiritual meekness that characterizes the Christian should not be confused with cowardice, however. God's meek people also have true Christian courage. The spiritual grace of meekness has, you could say, a Siamese twin—Christian boldness. Like Christ, the Lion-Lamb, His people have both a lion-like and lamb-like character.

The apostle Paul exemplified both these qualities in his life and ministry. He instructed Timothy not to "strive; but be gentle" (2 Tim. 2:24). But to the Thessalonians, he wrote, "We were bold in our God" (1 Thess. 2:2). You could say that, in a way, Paul's boldness was a result of his meekness. He leaned wholly on his God, who was his source of courage—enabling him to traverse the world, testify before rulers, and endure the buffetings of Satan.

At this point in their history, the Jews needed this same boldness in the face of opposition. In Ezra 5, we see the Lord giving them the courage they needed by coming to them with His word and giving them tokens of His care. Let's look more closely at the events of this chapter.

The Lord's Word

We saw at the end of chapter 4 that the Jews' enemies, having used a full arsenal of weapons, had succeeded in bringing the building project to a standstill. Now that the work had ceased, what was the way forward? Surprisingly, it was a *few words* that made a dramatic difference and showed them the way. Verse 1 reads: "Then the prophets, Haggai the prophet, and Zechariah the son of Iddo, prophesied unto the Jews that were in Judah and Jerusalem in the name of the God of Israel, even unto them." As a result, verse 2 tells us, Joshua and Zerubbabel immediately rose up to begin building again.

How are we to understand this sudden restart? Simply put, although Artaxerxes, the king of Persia, had ordered a halt to building, the King of heaven ordered something else! His messengers, Haggai and Zechariah, spoke in the "name of the God of Israel." Ambassadors from the throne room of God, these men did not try to encourage the people with their own ideas. In the end, a few words, spoken in the name of God by His prophets, pushed the enemy *back* and the work of the temple *forward*. Joshua and Zerubbabel responded to the prophets' words in faith as they rose up to build again.

Verse 2 tells us that the prophets helped in the work as it continued. We are given considerably more detail about how they helped in Haggai 1 and Zechariah 1. Basically, they spoke the word of God to the people. Zechariah 1:16 gives us a taste of God's message to the people: "Therefore thus saith the LORD; I am returned to Jerusalem with mercies: my house shall be built in it, saith the LORD of hosts, and a line shall be stretched forth upon Jerusalem." Do you see how the words these prophets spoke must have refreshed, challenged, comforted, and encouraged the Jews as they built? God's word is all-sufficient!

By nature, we underestimate the power of God's spoken word. Even if all those who oppose Him would unite in defiance against Him, one word from Him would be more than enough to destroy them. The psalmist says: "He uttered his voice, the earth melted" (46:6). Psalm 29 gives us an impressive description of what God's voice can do. For example, it "breaketh the cedars" (v. 5) and "shaketh the wilderness" (v. 8).

Today, many forces come against the church. How easily God's people underestimate the Lord's word! How quickly we look to the world for modern methods we can use to help the church's cause succeed or simply throw up our hands in resignation! But how slow we are to trust in the simple power of the Word of God! When will we learn that God's Word—the Bible—is the only weapon the church needs?

The Lord's Eye

Not much time passed before opposition came marching back onto the scene. This time it came in the form of Tatnai, the official governor of the large region of which Judah was part. With him came an intimidating entourage—Shetharboznai and "his companions" (v. 6). They demanded to know who had authorized this construction, took down names, and then made the matter an official case with King Darius, the successor of Artaxerxes (vv. 3–5).

This had the potential to be a tremendous setback. Basically, it amounted to filing a lawsuit against the Jews with the king himself! The Jews could easily have been overcome with discouragement by this turn of events. But, thankfully, we don't read that was the case. Instead, while the matter was pending, the building project continued. Apparently, for reasons not revealed, Tatnai had not gone so far as to officially put a stop to the building. This was, of course, in God's providence. We read in verse 5, "But the eye of their God was upon the elders of the Jews, that they could not cause them to cease."

How comforting for God's people to have the eye of the Lord upon them! Psalm 33:18–19 explains: "Behold, the eye of the LORD is upon them that fear him, upon them that hope in his mercy; to deliver their soul from death, and to keep them alive in famine." Psalm 34:15 says: "The eyes of the LORD are upon the righteous, and his ears are open unto their cry." When we look to Him for mercy, we can be assured that His eye will be upon us for Christ's sake!

The Lord's Service

As in the previous chapter, the rest of this chapter contains a number of official documents, which Ezra must have had access to as he wrote this book. The documents are basically a look into the dossier, or collection of documents, of the prosecutor (vv. 6–17). Essentially, in chapter 5, we have the request from Tatnai's entourage for Darius to pass judgment on the Jews. Why would the Lord have included these spiteful things from the enemy's pen in inspired Scripture? Let's look at them more closely, and we will find a number of helpful lessons.

First, notice that the Jews called themselves the *servants of God* (v. 11). Before Darius, his servants, and the world, these Jews readily identified themselves in this important way. They belonged to the "God of heaven and earth" (v. 11). As His servants, they intended to follow His leading and to wait upon His bidding. What a different spirit we see in these Jews from that which had characterized them before! They had forsaken this God in favor of their idols in the past. But those idols had shown themselves to be powerless gods, able only to bring down those who served them. Now the Jews were again content to serve the Lord alone.

The second thing we notice is that the Jews did not hide their sin from the king (v. 12). They tell him that their fathers had provoked God and that He had given them into Nebuchadnezzar's hand as a result. This is remarkable! This implies their admission that God had been just in all His dealings with them. They had learned what the prophet Micah had said: "I will bear the indignation of the LORD" (7:9). Subjected to the scrutiny and judgment of this Persian king, they testified of being subjected to the judgment of a greater, heavenly King!

How could the Jews continue their building under an assault like Tatnai's? What kept them from shaking off their responsibilities under such intense political pressure? This zeal did not come from within the Jews. In the previous chapter, we saw their hands hanging down. But now the Lord furnished them with what they needed. Their eagerness reminds us of the perfect eagerness of Christ, who said, "The zeal of thine house hath eaten me up" (John 2:17). The word of God, the eye of God, and the service of God strengthened these returning prodigals, enabling them to overcome their adversaries and all opposition.

Questions

1. Compare Haggai 1 and Zechariah 1 with Ezra 5:1. Besides Zechariah 1:16, which was quoted in this chapter, what else did God say through these prophets?

2. Both Ezra 4 and 5 show the Jews facing difficult opposition. How do they respond differently in chapter 5 than they did in chapter 4? What explains the difference?

3. What are some of the ways we fail to rely on the Word of God as we ought?

4. How can we know that God's eye is upon us in the special way we see in Ezra 5?

5. These elders seem to have given their names to Tatnai (v. 10). This must have been risky. Yet, in the end, it proved a great honor. How so?

6. What does it mean to bow under the righteous judgment of God? (See v. 12.) How does submission to God produce boldness in God?

~ 6 ~

JOY THROUGH GOD

Ezra 6

Let's summarize the story line thus far. God had awakened the Jews in exile to return to Him and to the worship of His name. In response to His call, they traveled a considerable distance from Babylon to Judah. Once back in their homeland, they faced challenges and opposition. Their enemies tempted them first by suggesting that they join forces. When this scheme didn't succeed, they tried other tactics, managing to stop the building temporarily. Yet, by His word, the Lord strengthened His people's hands and showed that His eye was on them. His love was drawing them to Himself, and nothing their enemies did could keep them from the joy that they were about to experience in Ezra 6.

Whenever God's people have a season of joy, it is because the Lord has worked by His grace. The people in this chapter certainly didn't deserve the blessings they received in a completed temple building. It wasn't their hard work or persevering attitude that brought them to this point. It wasn't their deeds that were worth celebrating. The psalmist said, "For thou, LORD, hast made me glad through thy work: I will triumph *in the works of thy hands*" (92:4, emphasis added). After years of work on God's house, these returning prodigals were to enjoy a season of sweet joy. They ascribed everything to God; He was the one who had brought things to this point. The last verse of chapter 6 so fittingly says, "For the LORD had made them joyful, and turned the heart of the king of Assyria unto them, to strengthen their hands in the work of the house of God, the God of Israel." Let's look more closely at the events of this chapter through the lens of this concluding verse.

The Lord Turned the King's Heart

As chapter 6 opens, the Jews are waiting to hear Darius's verdict regarding the building project. Their future was hanging in the balance! Some, likely, were understandably worried that Darius might turn against them. Other Jews may have clung to the word of God as He had spoken it through Isaiah, promising that the temple would be rebuilt (see Isa. 44:28).

The Lord rewarded this faith of His trusting servants. Upon Darius's order, a search was made, and record was found of Cyrus's original commission to the Jews. This was no coincidence. Instead, it was God's providence. God was turning the heart of Darius to accomplish His own purposes. Proverbs 21:1 says, "The king's heart is in the hand of the LORD." How clearly we see this truth in this instance! He brought Darius to issue the decree He had ordained. Let's look at what this decree accomplished.

First, through this decree, God made the adversaries cease their opposition. Darius addressed the enemies of the Jews very pointedly: "Let the work of this house of God alone" (v. 7). Second, God made even the adversaries help with supplies for building and offering. Darius instructed Tatnai: "That which they have need of…let it be given them day by day without fail" (v. 9). Third, God made the adversaries fear God's retribution upon any disobedience. Darius issued his own threat against any opposition (v. 11), but he also invoked God's judgment: "And the God that hath caused his name to dwell there destroy all kings and people, that shall put to their hand to alter and to destroy this house of God" (v. 12). The threat of divine judgment rested on those who would dare to interfere with the Jews' work.

There is no question that this decision dealt the Jews' enemies a heavy blow. Similar things have happened at other times in biblical history. When God brought the Israelites out of their captivity in Egypt, the Egyptians not only had to let Israel go, but they also gave spoils along with them (Ex. 12:36). Or think of Haman, who was forced to lead Mordecai on horseback through the city of Shushan (Est. 6:11). On these and other occasions, the adversaries of the people of God actually ended up helping rather than hurting them.

What a comfort this should be to the church! Its enemies might rage and threaten, yet, in the end, "the sons also of them that afflicted thee shall come bending unto thee" (Isa. 60:14). Truly, "no weapon that is formed against thee shall prosper" (Isa. 54:17).

He Strengthened His People's Hands

The king's edict not only confounded the adversaries' plans, but we are told that it also strengthened the Jews' hands (v. 22). This, of course, implies that the Jews, as courageous and zealous as they were, still were weak and in need of strength. Enmity had hindered them from the outside, but so had weakness on the inside.

Verse 14 gives us evidence of the Jews' hands being strengthened. Notice that in this verse, we have three verbs. The Jews "prospered," "builded," and "finished." Because of the strength the builders received from God, they were able to take the project to completion. The day came when the last brick was laid, the last piece of furniture installed, and the last tools put away. The long-awaited temple stood completed—a monument to God's strengthening grace!

Who does not need this strengthening grace? God's people are frequently buffeted, externally and internally, by adversaries of the gospel and a sense of their own weakness. Just as in this chapter God strengthened His people to build up the temple, so now God continues to strengthen His people in holiness through the preaching of the Word. When we seek strength from Him, then we will also be strengthened with might in the inner man (Eph. 3:16). As Paul confessed: "I can do all things through Christ which strengtheneth me" (Phil. 4:13).

He Gladdened His People's Hearts

God's work on His people's behalf resulted in joy and gladness. This passage uses the word "joy" and "joyful" three times (vv. 16–22). We could define true joy as a settled, inward posture of gladness in God, which has its source in God the Holy Spirit (Gal. 5:22). This joy comes from God and is focused on Him.

What joy there must have been when the Jews dedicated the temple to the Lord (vv. 16–17)! They gave back to God what He had given to them. It was to be *His* house. They sacrificed hundreds of animals; after seventy years, the blood that spoke of reconciliation began to flow again. It pointed forward to Jesus Christ and His one sacrifice for sin. By it, He would consecrate the whole house of God and all His people.

What joy there must have been when the people reinstituted the regular service of the Lord (v. 18)! After all these decades of being without the temple, these priests and the Levites could take up their duties and mediate between God and the people.

What joy also there must have been when the people could celebrate the Passover once again (vv. 19–21)! This festival reminded the people of their deliverance from Pharaoh, their cruel enemy. And now, they could not only celebrate their deliverance from Egypt, but they could also celebrate the Lord's faithfulness in delivering them from their enemies! Based on their experience, they could say with the psalmist: "But thou hast saved us from our enemies, and hast put them to shame that hated us" (44:7). His name was to be glorified!

This chapter points out that the people who celebrated on this special day were those who had "separated themselves unto them from the filthiness of the heathen of the land, to seek the LORD God of Israel" (v. 21). What an exact description of the very point on which we have been focusing! These people knew the reality of true repentance. Like the prodigal of Christ's parable, these people once had joined with the wicked in their sin in the far country of Babylon. But through the Lord's mercy and love, they had separated themselves and returned to Him. You could say of these people what Peter said of the Christians to whom he wrote many centuries later:

they had "escaped the corruption that is in the world through lust" (2 Peter 1:4). Elsewhere, he puts it like this: "For ye were as sheep going astray; but are now returned unto the Shepherd and Bishop of your souls" (1 Peter 2:25).

It's no wonder that for such prodigals, there would be great joy and gladness in the house of the Lord. Just as the father of Christ's parable greeted the returning prodigal with a joyful feast (Luke 15:22–24), these returning prodigals were entering into the joy of the Lord. Such joy is not the result of our works, but rather of God's deeds (see Ps. 92:4). As the last verse of Ezra 6 says, it was the Lord who made them joyful!

Questions

1. In what way could Ezra 6 be called an emblem of God's faithfulness?

2. Darius's decree was advantageous for the Jews and disadvantageous for their enemies. Can you think of other times in history, other than those mentioned in this chapter, when God's enemies were made to serve His cause?

3. The Lord's people need God's strength every step of the way. By what means does God usually provide this strength? Where do we see this in the passage?

4. What is true joy? Can you give examples of false joy? Can you think of someone you know (or have known) who has obviously had true joy? How does/did that person demonstrate that joy?

5. What is verse 21 describing, spiritually speaking? Compare this with Ephesians 2:1–3.

A FURTHER REFORMATION

Ezra 7

About fifty-six years passed between the events of Ezra 6 and those of chapter 7. This early period after the exile was a memorable time. Important advances had been made, victories won, and challenges overcome. Joy had come because of what God had graciously done. However, the accomplishments celebrated in chapter 6 did not signal the end of what God would do in His people. The history in the rest of Ezra and in Nehemiah will recount more instances of God's continuing work. His people would continue to have a sinful nature, and they would continue to need further reformation.

As a record of His will and way, God's Word is the chief means by which the Lord advances His cause of reformation. That is what we will see in these next chapters. Though the Jews had enjoyed a spiritual awakening more than fifty years earlier, they were in need of a fresh outpouring of grace. God raised up Ezra to use him in bringing reforming grace. Ezra was a "man of *the* book"—namely, the Scriptures. With God's Word, he traveled from Babylon to the community already established in Judah. The Word touched the people's hearts. They were humbled as they saw their sin, and their lives were changed through the Word's power.

The Pure Word of God

It is important to notice at the start that there can be no reformation without submission to the Word of God. This chapter contains many references to God's Word, using the phrase "the law of the God of heaven" (vv. 12, 21) and other related terminology. What is reformation, other than bringing the *church* of God back in line with the *Word* of God in doctrine, life, and worship? Today we often hear, "The church must be always reforming," a statement with which we should wholeheartedly agree. Some people, however, mean by this that the church should always be adapting to changing times. What reform really involves, though, is constantly returning to the Word of God. Any development that doesn't bring the church into closer subjection to the Word of God is not reformation, but deformation.

The Bible calls Ezra "a ready scribe in the law of Moses, which the LORD God of Israel had given" (v. 6). This means that he was highly skilled in understanding the law that God had given to His people through Moses. Undoubtedly, Ezra had spent a good part of his life studying this law. As the children of Israel were deported into exile, someone must have taken scrolls of the law along. Perhaps Ezra had spent a lot of time copying it. He certainly had made it his life's work to know the Word of God thoroughly. So although the people were away from the temple, they still had access to God's law. As a child of the captivity, he could have identified with what we read in Psalm 119:54: "Thy statutes have been my songs in the house of my pilgrimage."

We read that "Ezra had prepared his heart to seek the law of the LORD, and to do it, and to teach in Israel statutes" (v. 10). The order of the words in this verse is noteworthy: "seek," "do," and "teach." It was certainly important for Ezra to be highly trained in God's Word. But, more importantly, he submitted to it with mind, heart, and strength. He went beyond seeking God's Word to doing it. His was not a heartless, or intellectual, study of the Word of God; he studied with a heart prepared to heed the Word. Whether he knew this prayer of David or not, he lived it: "Teach me, O LORD, the way of thy statutes; and I will keep it unto the end. Give me understanding, and I shall keep thy law; yea, I shall observe it with my whole heart" (Ps. 119:33–34).

Only after seeking and doing God's law was Ezra qualified to teach it. He was not like the hypocritical scribes against whom Christ warned: "Do not ye after their works: for they say, and do not" (Matt. 23:3). God had worked obedience and submission in Ezra's heart and then used Ezra to bring about obedience and submission to the Word in His people's hearts.

The Powerful Hand of God

God's protecting and directing hand of providence accomplishes reformation in His people. This chapter refers to the hand of God (vv. 6, 9, 28). The Bible frequently mentions God's hand (see, for example, Ex. 13:3; Ruth 1:13; 1 Sam. 5:6; Ps. 118:15). The Heidelberg Catechism appropriately and beautifully connects God's hand to His providence, saying that "all creatures are so in His hand, that without His will they cannot so much as move" (Lord's Day 10, question 28). The Bible usually refers to the hand of God when it speaks of His providential acts of judgment against His enemies and salvation for His people.

In verse 6, the hand of the Lord is seen as that which directed the king to grant Ezra "all his request." Verses 11–26 detail how Artaxerxes provided Ezra with everything necessary for the work in Jerusalem, as if he were giving Ezra a blank check. God was providing for His people's support, even through the hands of unbelievers around them—a common theme in the books of Ezra and Nehemiah. Ezra gives the Lord's good hand the credit for this.

Second, the hand of God protected Ezra on his journey (v. 9). Over the span of four months (vv. 8–9), God proved to be the One who watched over His people and kept them safe (see Ps. 121:5). Keep in mind that the journey from Babylon to Jerusalem would not have been a safe or easy one. Many dangers could have befallen them, yet none did. Ezra confessed that it was the "good hand of his God" that brought him safely to Jerusalem (v. 9).

Third, the hand of God provided a whole company of people to go with Ezra. Ezra mentions this explicitly in verse 28: "And I was strengthened as the hand of the LORD my God was upon me, and I gathered together out of Israel chief men to go up with me." Among them were officers—priests, Levites, singers, porters, Nethinim, and other important men. Unseen by human eyes, God's hand gathered a remnant to return with Ezra, like a shepherd gathers and leads His flock (see Ps. 77:20).

No wonder Ezra felt constrained to praise and thank God for the work of His hand! Like David in the well-known Shepherd Psalm, he certainly saw God's "goodness and mercy" following him (see Ps. 23:6). Ezra explicitly mentions God's goodness in verse 9 and His mercy in verse 28. This same providence of God governs and directs our every step in life. Do we, like Ezra, see goodness and mercy in it?

In summary, Ezra experienced the hand of the Lord as a source of strength. He focuses on this strength of God's hand when he writes in verse 28: "I was *strengthened* as the hand of the LORD my God was upon me" (emphasis added). He experienced what Isaiah had written: "Trust ye in the LORD for ever: for in the LORD JEHOVAH is everlasting strength" (26:4). Similarly, David said, "Thou hast a mighty arm: strong is thy hand, and high is thy right hand" (Ps. 89:13). The true secret to strength for each day is to lean on the strength of Almighty God in Jesus Christ. There, His strength is made perfect in our weakness (see 2 Cor. 12:9). If we desire to see a time of reformation, we should look for it only from the hand of the Lord.

The Beautiful House of God

What was God's purpose in sending His Word and extending His hand? He was reforming His Zion—or, to use the picturesque language of this chapter, He was working to "beautify" His house (v. 27). In our fallen world, everything is subject to decay, even God's church on earth. Just as we periodically need to renovate and refurnish our homes, so, too, God beautifies His house, and He does so by His Word and hand.

How did He beautify His house in this chapter? As we already saw, Artaxerxes sent along an abundance of supply out of his own treasury house (vv. 15–23). The king relinquished "all the silver and gold" that Ezra could find (v. 16), "and whatsoever more shall be needful for the house of thy God" (v. 20). It's part of God's amazing plan that He utilizes and consecrates the riches of the Gentiles to serve the praise of His glory. What Isaiah had prophesied was being fulfilled: "The glory of Lebanon shall come unto thee, the fir tree, the pine tree, and the box together, to *beautify* the place of my sanctuary; and I will make the place of my feet glorious" (60:13, emphasis added). God was doing something similar to what He had done a generation or two before, as recorded in Ezra 1, when the first people returned from Babylon.

We are not sure why the Lord's house needed beautification. Perhaps it had fallen into disrepair over the first decades after its rebuilding. Or perhaps the Jews now had more resources at their disposal than they had originally had. Whatever the case, we should look beyond the physical circumstances for the spiritual lesson here. Because the church is made up of sinners, the Lord's *spiritual* house quickly falls into a dilapidated condition. Every generation needs to experience the beautifying work of the Lord in reformation and revival (see Ps. 90:17). Ultimately, God does not beautify His church and people by external ornamentation. Remember that Ezra's ministry was deeply Word-centered. As the Lord brings His Word to bear on hearts and lives, His house is beautified.

God beautifies His church so that He may dwell in it. We read that Christ gave Himself for His church in order that "he might sanctify and cleanse it with the washing of water by the word, that he might present it to himself a glorious church, not having spot, or wrinkle, or any such thing; but that it should be holy and without blemish" (Eph. 5:26–27). The glorious hope of the people of God is that one day there will be no more need for reformation, for the new Jerusalem shall come down from God out of heaven, "prepared" and "adorned" (Rev. 21:2).

Until that day, however, God will continue to shape, fashion, and mold His church by His Word and by His hand. May He give us a Word-centered heart like Ezra's! Our hope for reformation does not rest in human might, but in the subduing power of the gospel of the Lord Jesus Christ. Through His Son and the power of His right hand, He gives "beauty for ashes, the oil of joy for mourning…that he might be glorified" (Isa. 61:3).

Questions

1. Find five verses in Psalm 119 (other than the ones listed in this chapter) that give voice to Ezra's main aim in life as we read it in Ezra 7:10.

2. What are ways we could prepare our hearts to seek the law of God (Ezra 7:10)?

3. The Persian king called the law of God "the wisdom of thy God" (v. 25). He also saw that there would be wrath from heaven if God's law were not obeyed (v. 23). How do you explain that the king outside the church had such high esteem for God's Word, whereas many inside the church today have such low esteem for it?

4. Can we still discern the hand of God like Ezra did? What are some things that point to the hand of God in the church or in our lives?

5. How did Ezra respond to evidences of the hand of God? What posture does this teach us with respect to God's providence?

6. Ezra was raised up for a unique task. But still, Ezra should be a powerful model for us today. What can we learn from him? Also discuss how Ezra is a picture of Christ.

~ 8 ~

A FRESH EXODUS

Ezra 8

Traveling involves certain risks and uncertainties. We don't know what we will encounter along the way, whether our trip will be safe, or whether we will arrive at our destination on time. In this chapter, we see Ezra assembling a fresh group of Jews who would return from captivity. They would embark on this hazardous journey to Jerusalem and arrive safely. This company of Jews had no human army to protect them from dangers they might encounter, but they did have their Divine Guard with them. They put their faith in Him, and that faith was not put to shame.

Assembling the Tribes for the Journey

Ezra 8 records the names and family connections of the people returning to the Land of Promise with Ezra. It's worth noting how this list is formatted. The priestly and royal families—those of Phinehas, Ithamar, and David—are mentioned first (v. 2). Then follow the names of twelve families, with the number of males from each family. The number twelve suggests the twelve tribes of Israel, though we don't know whether each family was from a different tribe or which tribe each family represented. Together, the men from these families totaled about fifteen hundred people. Once women and children were factored in, the number would be more like five thousand.

As a careful and concerned leader, Ezra took time to gather and "view," or inspect, the people who would join him on the journey home (v. 15). He noticed that though there were priests included, he "found there none of the sons of Levi" (v. 15). Ezra obviously knew that the Levites had been appointed to assist the priests in the worship of God. Their absence would leave the returning company without qualified servants for worship.

Ezra addressed this problem by sending a delegation to Iddo, a chief at Casiphia. The phrase "the place Casiphia" (v. 17) is noteworthy in the original Hebrew. There may have been an early synagogue at Casiphia or perhaps a training school for Levites and Nethinim. The Nethinim, a class of temple servants, are mentioned only in the books of Ezra and Nehemiah and once in Chronicles (1 Chron. 9:2). Apparently, they were assistants to the Levites, who, in turn, assisted the priests.

According to verses 18–20, Ezra's men brought back Levites and Nethinim from Casiphia to join the group of travelers—about forty Levites and 220 Nethinim. Now they had men among them who could fulfill the divinely appointed role of a mediating and ministering tribe on their behalf. In his record, Ezra highlights one of them, Sherebiah, whom he called "a man of understanding" (v. 18). What a gift even one man or woman of understanding is to a group of people! By faith, Ezra saw that this was the "good hand of our God upon us" (v. 18).

If Sherebiah was such an encouragement to Ezra, how much more should we adore God's good hand in His provision of Jesus Christ? In Christ are hidden "all the treasures of wisdom and knowledge" (Col. 2:3). As He went about His Father's business, the scribes were "astonished at his understanding" (Luke 2:47). Through Him, God's hand is still at work today. We may worry because the church appears small in number, and true ministers are hard to find. Yet God's gracious hand will gather in every one of His children. His 144,000 are sealed and will all be brought in without fail (Rev. 7:4–8).

Escaping the Dangers of the Journey

In this chapter, Ezra was faced with the daunting prospect of a dangerous journey. Considering the perils of wilderness travel, a military escort would not have been unreasonable. However, Ezra knew he had to practice what he had preached. Before the king, he had spoken of God's good hand, which "is upon all them for good that seek him." Could he let the king think that he needed more protection than that good hand would provide? He was "ashamed" to ask for more than that (v. 22).

Let's examine our lives for a moment. Do we send a consistent message to those around us like Ezra did here? Do we perhaps speak of God's power but at the same time show that we are leaning on human strength? Like Ezra, believers know the struggle between faith and unbelief in their lives. In the end, though, God upheld Ezra's faith, and it shone brightly in witness to the king. He refused to ask for more than the Lord's help.

It is important to notice that this victory of faith did not come without some fasting and prayer. Ezra called for corporate humiliation by the river of Ahava, "to seek of him a right way for us" (v. 21). Like his forefather Jacob, who feared the armies of his brother, Esau, on his journey back to Canaan, Ezra "wept, and made supplication" to God (Hos. 12:4). Like Jacob, he entered the land unassailed by his foes.

Still today, God's people can encounter many enemies on their journey to their heavenly country (see Heb. 11:16). Whether these enemies persecute the church or lead it astray through false doctrine, the only way forward is to look to the Lord. Ezra experienced what the psalmist celebrated: "He shall cover thee with his feathers, and under his wings shalt thou trust: his truth shall be thy shield and buckler. Thou shalt not be afraid for the terror by night; nor for the arrow that flieth by day; nor for the pestilence that walketh in darkness; nor for the destruction that wasteth at noonday" (91:4–6).

Transporting the Treasures during the Journey

If you had happened upon this group of pilgrims traveling through the wilderness to Jerusalem, the sight would have been impressive—five thousand people walking unarmed. Among them was a group of twelve priests and Levites who were charged with a sacred task: transporting gold, silver, and temple vessels for use in the temple (vv. 24–30). Ezra explained: "Ye are holy unto the LORD; the vessels are holy also" (v. 28). As long ago the Levites had carried the ark of the Lord through the wilderness and across the Jordan, so now Levites carried these sacred things as they returned to the land (see Josh. 3:3). Great care had to be taken so that these important implements and furnishings would arrive safely in Jerusalem (vv. 24–30). The Levites' special task was to "watch" and "keep" (v. 29); carelessness and negligence would be cardinal sins (see 2 Sam. 6:6–7). When they arrived in Jerusalem, every implement would be counted and every piece of precious metals weighed, just as Ezra had meticulously counted and weighed it all before entrusting it to the care of the priests and Levites (vv. 25–26, 29, 33).

These priests and Levites were entrusted with the valuable things pertaining to the *earthly* temple of God. Looking beyond them, we see that Christ, the fulfillment of all the Old Testament ceremonies, was entrusted with the valuable things pertaining to the *heavenly* temple of God. He faithfully bore His people close to His heart like stones in his priestly breastplate. He could give account to His Father of His sacred charge: "While I was with them in the world, I kept them in thy name" (John 17:12).

The Lord's people also have precious things entrusted to them. For example, Paul wrote to Timothy, his spiritual son: "O Timothy, keep that which is committed to thy trust" (1 Tim. 6:20). Elsewhere he writes, "Hold fast the form of sound words, which thou hast heard of me, in faith and love which is in Christ Jesus" (2 Tim. 1:13). None of us can say that we have not been entrusted with precious things, such as the Word of God. We will also have to give account of the things with which we have been blessed. May we, by grace, be diligent to use them rightly, with God's blessing!

Questions

1. How does this chapter illustrate the importance of families in the cause of God?

2. Sherebiah is called a "man of understanding" (v. 18). What does the Bible mean by the word "understanding"? (See Ex. 36:1; Deut. 4:6; 1 Kings 3:9; Ps. 119:130, 144.)

3. Trace Ezra's struggle between fear and faith in this chapter. How real is this in the Christian life? What light do the Psalms shed on this struggle? (See Ps. 56.)

4. Is there any place for corporate humiliation today? Read Joel 2:15–17 and reflect on its significance today.

5. What are some treasures we must "watch and keep" today? What can we learn from Ezra's carefulness on this point?

6. Read Psalm 121. What might this psalm have meant to Ezra on his journey? How does it apply to the life of faith today?

A TIME FOR BROKENNESS

Ezra 9

Based on what we learned in chapter 8, we might expect that Ezra would have immediately set himself to teaching the law or beautifying the temple. Those had been the main aims of Ezra's mission to Jerusalem. Yet when we turn to chapters 9 and 10 of Ezra, we see something very different. Had something happened to sideline Ezra's mission? Had his plans been forgotten?

We could compare Ezra's actions in chapters 9 and 10 to those of a carpenter who is renovating a home. Perhaps you have had an experience similar to the one we had. My wife and I decided we wanted to replace a linoleum floor in the bathroom of an older home that we had purchased. One of our relatives began working on the project. But when he lifted up the linoleum, he found that some of the floorboards underneath had rotted and would need replacing. In the end, the renovation went to a deeper level and took longer than we had anticipated. But that is what some renovations require. This is similar to the situation in which Ezra found himself. The work he had anticipated doing was necessary, but the problem went deeper than he had thought. The "rot" that had occurred was too invasive to be ignored.

In spiritual life, the rot of sin always goes deeper than it looks. We might be tempted to turn a blind eye to deeper issues and just deal with sin on the surface level. But what is on the surface is only the tip of the iceberg of a deeper problem. We may try, like Adam, to patch things over with fig leaves, but such a cover-up will not withstand God's scrutiny. And so, in this chapter, Ezra found that nothing short of a complete overhaul would do.

Brokenness Required because of Spiritual Compromise

In verses 1 and 2, we read that the princes gave Ezra bad news. The people of Israel had not separated themselves from the surrounding nations and their sins. They had mixed with them through intermarriages. Sadly, the princes and rulers had led the way in this sin (v. 2).

God had not specifically forbidden all marriages between Jews and those of other nationalities. Notable cases of intermarriage included Moses and Zipporah, Salmon and Rahab, and Boaz and Ruth. Instead, the problem was intermarriage with *idolaters.* Moses had warned the Israelites about the indigenous people of the land of Canaan (Deut. 7:1–6) and the Egyptians (see Lev. 18:3) because of their idolatrous worship. Marriages with such people resulted in unfaithfulness to God. The people's compromise in this area meant that the whole foundation of the nation's life was being compromised. This was no surface problem with a quick fix!

Even though we no longer live in a time when God's special dealings are tied to a particular land, the sin of compromise is always near. In our age, the spirit of compromise runs rampant. Ours is a time of pervasive unfaithfulness to God and disobedience to His Word. If we are going to understand the depth of the problem, we need to understand how compromise threatens us. People argue persuasively in favor of accommodating other belief systems and worldviews. Probably all of us have heard arguments like these: "We need to cooperate with people in order to impact them"; "We shouldn't stick out like a sore thumb"; "You can't hide your head in the sand"; "We need to be there so we can redeem our culture"; or, "If you don't change, you will lose the next generation."

Scripture does not command us to live in monasteries or separated communities like the Amish do. But Paul did exhort: "Come out from among them, and be ye separate, saith the Lord, and touch not the unclean thing; and I will receive you" (2 Cor. 6:17). Just as the Jews in this chapter needed to separate themselves from the pagan idolaters and take a stand of separation on the principles of God's Word, Christians today must follow Scripture as our only guide. Just as the floorboards underneath the linoleum were rotting, the foundation of the household of faith will rot if we fail to separate ourselves from the world.

Brokenness Demonstrated in Thorough Humiliation

Verse 3 tells us how Ezra responded after he heard about the people's sins; he rent his clothes and mantle, plucked hair from his head and beard, and sat down in astonishment. Verse 4 tells us that Ezra was joined by other God-fearing

Jews. He sat astonished until the time for the evening sacrifice, then rose up, fell on his knees, and spread out his hands unto God (vv. 4–5). These were signs of deep grief and mourning, similar to the expressions of a person whose loved one had died (see Job 1:20; Isa. 22:12; Ezek. 7:18).

The cause for Ezra's mourning, however, was something even more serious than physical death. When he finally arose from his "heaviness," or visible demonstration of humiliation (v. 5), he explained his actions in prayer: "Our iniquities are increased over our head, and our trespass is grown up unto the heavens" (v. 6). Worse than death is sin against God, for it deserves death! This explains Ezra's deep humiliation. He understood that this was not the time so much for burnt offerings; it was a time for brokenness. As David said, "The sacrifices of God are a broken spirit: a broken and a contrite heart, O God, thou wilt not despise" (Ps. 51:17). These are the things that Ezra offered to God.

Thorough humiliation is not easy. It is far easier and more comfortable to heal the wound on the surface than to open it wide. But the Bible warns us that our repentance must be more than a "morning cloud" or the "early dew" (Hos. 6:4). What we need instead is heartfelt brokenness over sin. Let's look at three lessons we can learn from Ezra's brokenness.

First, when we are broken because of our sin, we regard sin as *heinous*. Ezra acknowledged: "I am ashamed and blush" (v. 6). There was something detestable about the people's sins; they had reached into the heavens and polluted the land with uncleanness (vv. 6, 11). Do we see the horrendous character of our sins like Ezra did?

Second, when we are broken because of our sin, we acknowledge sin as *unreasonable*. It is committed against a good-doing God. How can we make any reasonable excuses for it? Sin cannot be justified. It is inexcusable and wicked in light of who God is. For example, Ezra pointed out that God had given the Jews "a nail in his holy place" (v. 8). In this instance, "nail" means a tent peg. He is saying that God has given them a place to pitch their tent in their earthly journey. What had the people returned to God for this kind hospitality but sin? Ezra emphasized how unreasonable the people's sin had been when he asked, "And now, O our God, what shall we say after this?" (v. 10). Later, he asked, "Should we again break thy commandments?" (v. 14).

Third, when we are broken because of our sin, we acknowledge sin as *devastating*. Ezra understood that sin had terrible consequences. It incurs the just and complete anger of God (v. 14). God would have been righteous if He had wiped Israel completely from the earth. Whether God punishes immediately or waits for a later day to judge, we must always remember that the consequences of sin will be death. Justice delayed is never justice denied. In light of what the nation's sin deserved, it was impossible for Ezra to minimize things. He sought a repentance that was as deep as it was broad.

Brokenness Concluding in Divine Vindication

We may find it surprising that Ezra's prayer does not end with any specific plea. We might have expected a plea for mercy, pardon, and deliverance. But verse 15 simply reads: "O LORD God of Israel, thou art righteous: for we remain yet escaped, as it is this day: behold, we are before thee in our trespasses: for we cannot stand before thee because of this." Ezra's prayer was not a patchwork prayer, seeking restoration without true brokenness. And so he ended his prayer by declaring God to be in the right. He demonstrated in his prayer what Paul would later describe: "that every mouth may be stopped, and all the world may become guilty before God" (Rom. 3:19). This is not a fatalistic resignation. Rather, it is a faith that rests in God and His revealed character: "O LORD God of Israel, thou art righteous" (v. 15). Ezra's posture here is one of humble and holy rest in God.

In the end, Ezra's prayer ultimately calls for Calvary. At the cross of Christ, God proved that He could be righteous by laying the iniquity of His people on His Son, so that sinners could be declared righteous on the basis of Christ's righteousness. Ezra could mourn for sin. Christ alone could pay for sin. For Christ's sake, sinners can plead the glorious harmony of all God's attributes and find salvation.

Questions

1. Name some areas in which we can find ourselves engaged in spiritual compromise. Give practical examples of how we should be separate from this world.

2. Read verse 4. What characterized the people who joined Ezra? Compare Isaiah 66:2. What does it mean to tremble at God's word?

3. Ezra expresses shame and confusion on account of sin (vv. 6–7). Contrast Ezra's attitude with what we read in Zephaniah 3:5. Why was Ezra so sensitized to sin?

4. What are the sacrifices of God? How did Ezra offer them? Why are we so often content with "patch-work" repentance?

5. Compare Psalm 51:4 and Ezra 9:15. How do the two relate?

~ 10 ~

BREAKING WITH SIN

Ezra 10

In the previous chapter, we saw Ezra broken because of sin. But along with brokenness *over* sin should come breaking *with* sin. Mourning over sin, by itself, falls short of true conversion. As the Heidelberg Catechism explains, we must "hate and flee from" sin (Lord's Day 33, answer 89). Paul explained that "godly sorrow worketh repentance" (2 Cor. 7:10). This repentance involves a turning from sin. In Ezra 9, the people joined Ezra in mourning over their sin of intermarriage with the surrounding people. Now, in chapter 10, we see them breaking with their sin.

Essentially, Ezra 10 shows us prodigals demonstrating true repentance. We see how repentance began with the *heart*, as the people wept before the Lord (v. 1); then it moved to the *lips*, as they pledged obedience to the Lord (v. 12); then, finally, it moved to the *hand*, as they signed their names to do what the Lord commanded (v. 19). They showed that true repentance involves the whole person.

Repentance of Heart

Verse 1 tells us that "a very great congregation of men and women and children" wept bitterly. The people had sinned against God's grace and provoked His great wrath (9:8; 10:14). Through Ezra's leadership and godly example, they had become conscious of their sin. Their hearts had been broken as they heard Ezra pour out his heart before the Lord, vindicating His righteousness.

Not long before this took place, the prophet Zechariah had prophesied that the Lord would pour forth the spirit of grace and supplications, and the people would "mourn" and be "in bitterness" (12:10–14). Such tears of sorrow are a hopeful sign. Shechaniah said to Ezra: "Yet now there is hope in Israel concerning this thing" (v. 2). But it is important to remember that, by themselves, tears are not an infallible sign of true repentance (see Heb. 12:17). Rather, it is the heart behind the tears that God discerns. God does not despise "a broken and a contrite heart" (Ps. 51:17). According to Psalm 56, God even promises that He collects such heartfelt tears into His bottle and writes them in His book (v. 8). How important it is that our hearts would be affected by our sin and bring about true, heartfelt repentance!

Repentance of Lips

The second part of the people's repentance involved public confession. According to our chapter, Shechaniah took the lead in this. He called for a national covenant with God to annul these illegitimate marriages (v. 3). Ezra led in this by securing the cooperation of the chief priests, Levites, and all of Israel (v. 5). A proclamation was made that all who wished to join this national covenant should come to Jerusalem at a set time (vv. 7–8). Despite heavy rains, the people gathered together in response to this proclamation (v. 9). Ezra stood up, calling for a public confession from the people and an agreement to the covenant (v. 11).

What follows is significant: "Then all the congregation answered and said with a loud voice, As thou hast said, so must we do" (v. 12). The people publicly submitted themselves to the Lord's perfect will. As Ezra had said, they were obliged to "do his pleasure" (v. 11).

This is the language of true surrender and submission. It is such a significant part of genuine repentance. Without it, we will never be able to truly pray what Christ taught us to pray: "Thy will be done" (Matt. 6:10). Like the people in this chapter, we need to renounce our own will, resolving by grace to obey God's will without murmuring (see Heidelberg Catechism, answer 124).

Notice that this was done in a public setting, before many witnesses. Perhaps you did this when you made public confession of faith before the congregation in your church. In the Reformed church order, there are times when public confession of guilt is required; a repentant sinner pledges to forsake a particular sin and live in accordance with God's commandments in the future. Repentance can also involve less formal confessions of sin. For example, we should ask forgiveness from those we have wronged and admit to them that we have sinned. James encourages public confession when he writes: "Confess your faults one to another" (5:16). Public confession involves acknowledging our sin before men because we know ourselves to be sinners before God. This is the kind of confession we see in Ezra 10.

Repentance of Hands

The third part of the Jews' repentance in this chapter involved actual obedience. It's noteworthy that the text here specifically mentions the Jews' hands: "And they gave their hands that they would put away their wives" (v. 19). This wasn't a matter of only hearts and lips. Their repentance went further; they signed a document with their hands. They also used their hands to offer a sacrifice: "They offered a ram of the flock for their trespass" (v. 19). They followed through with their pledges.

People have a hard time understanding why Ezra would have stipulated that these foreign wives be sent away. This seems severe and even unbiblical. Doesn't God say explicitly that He hates divorce, as we read in Malachi 2:16? This is a good question worthy of a closer look, all the more because Malachi prophesied either shortly before or during Ezra's time. When we put Malachi 2:11–16 alongside Ezra's account, we can piece together what was actually happening:

1. Malachi accused Judah and Jerusalem of having "profaned the holiness" of the Lord by marrying "the daughter of a strange god" (2:11). Clearly, then, these intermarriages were resulting in idolatry within the congregation.

2. In the process of marrying these idolatrous wives, the people had been divorcing their original Jewish wives. Malachi mentions "the wife of [their] youth," whom they had treated treacherously (2:14).

In other words, they had been unfaithful to their proper wives in favor of these idolatrous wives. It must have become fashionable for men to put away their Jewish wife and marry someone from outside the community of faith. In Nehemiah 6:18, we read of alliances between people in Judah and those from outside that were sealed by marriages between the families. In other words, just as Solomon would make alliances with other nations and take wives from their royal families, so these Jews were sealing their agreements with outside families by marriages (see Neh. 13:26).

3. When God declared his hatred of divorce (Mal. 2:16), He had in mind the original marriage between a Jewish man and woman, which certain Jews were abandoning in favor of these new arrangements.

Indeed, God hates divorce. That is precisely why Ezra called the people to put away their idolatrous wives and return to the wives of their youth. The only way back was for those who had offended God's law and broken their original vows to disannul their secondary vows and keep their original ones.

The Jews in this chapter showed a full and true repentance. It was a repentance that began inwardly and worked its way outwardly in a breaking with sin. These people returned to the Lord and their covenant with Him. We should mark well that inward repentance without outward manifestations is incomplete repentance. And outward repentance that is not accompanied by inward repentance is mere hypocrisy. In repenting to the Lord, Israel was recommitting itself, as it were, to the marriage they held with the Lord. This relationship obliged them to forsake their former ways and cleave wholly unto the Lord.

God was willing to receive His returning bride, even though she had sinned against Him so grievously. If you belong to the bride of Christ, what a wonder it should be to you that He has wed you to Himself. How we need the Holy Spirit, that we might be quick in heart, lips, and hand to recommit ourselves to our "first love" (Rev. 2:4).

Questions

1. Why does unfaithfulness to God often show itself in human relationships, such as marriage and family?

2. The people wept bitterly under a sense of God's fierce wrath. Do we still understand the adverb "bitterly" and the adjective "fierce"? How do the two go together? How can there be "hope" here (v. 2)?

3. What is the role of leaders in the Christian church in issues of corporate repentance? What did the leaders do in this chapter?

4. What does it mean to do the Lord's pleasure (v. 11)?

5. Review how Malachi 2:11–16 helps shed light on Ezra 10.

6. What is Paul's instruction for believers who are married to unbelievers (1 Cor. 7:12–17)?

11

ON HIS KNEES BEFORE
THE COURT OF HEAVEN

Nehemiah 1

As the king's cupbearer, Nehemiah occupied one of the most prestigious positions in the Persian Empire. He would have been the envy of many. He walked in halls and rooms like none other in the world. The food he ate and the wine he drank were exquisite. But no matter how posh his surroundings, Nehemiah knew of a more excellent "court," to which he would retreat during free moments in his day and throughout the silent watches of the night (v. 6). There he found not lavishness, but holiness; not extravagance, but omnipotence; not delicacies, but mercies. This was the court of the King of heaven.

Burdened because of Ruined Zion

When Hanani, one of Nehemiah's relatives, came to see him, Nehemiah specifically asked about two things: first, about the remnant left in Jerusalem and, second, about the city itself. The answer that he received grieved him greatly (v. 4). Things were not good.

Like David in Psalm 122:9, Nehemiah delighted in the welfare of God's cause, Zion. So like his spiritual forefather,

Jeremiah, Nehemiah was hurt for the hurt of the daughter of his people (Jer. 8:21). How could he not be moved by the sad state of Jerusalem? How would he be able to go about his daily work without being burdened by this sad news?

How is the cause of God faring around you? Are God's people thriving or languishing? Are Zion's defenses secure, or are they in danger? When we look out over our local congregations and denominations, don't we often have to echo Hanani? Isn't the church often in a very needy condition? And when it is, do we then share Nehemiah's grief and concern as well? Nehemiah was lamenting the physical ruin of a city and looking after the physical welfare of the Lord's people. How much more should we be concerned about and grieve over the Lord's cause when it is suffering and seek after the spiritual well-being of His people?

Seeking Audience with Heaven's King

On hearing the news about Jerusalem's condition, Nehemiah did not quickly work out a plan of action with Hanani. He did not call together local Jews to form an action committee or to raise funds. He did not first bring the situation to the attention of the Persian king. Instead, he sought the hearing ear of God in heaven. Why go to humans when the divine ear is always open and attentive to the cries of the contrite? God is always able to move the wheels of providence however He sees fit. So often we go to prayer only when all else fails. Nehemiah shows us that prayer should not be a final resort but something we should see as an eminent privilege.

Nehemiah addressed God with great reverence: "O LORD God of heaven, the great and terrible God, that keepeth covenant and mercy for them that love him and observe his commandments" (v. 5). Though he did not mention Christ, we can say that here Nehemiah was approaching God in the name of Christ. How do we know? Notice that Nehemiah appealed on the one hand to the holiness of the "great and terrible" God and on the other hand to the covenant-keeping mercy of God. He did not separate God's holiness from His mercy; instead, the way he addressed God intertwined the two. And where, other than in Christ, do God's holiness and mercy come together so perfectly? In Christ, God is both holy and merciful for a poor sinner like Nehemiah. In Christ, there is access to the throne of God. And only because of Christ, we can make our prayer to the holy and merciful God.

Notice that Nehemiah was seeking God's attentive ear and His open eyes (v. 6). In other words, he was seeking God's face. He wanted his prayer to reach the ear of divine mercy and to be seen with the eyes of divine love. Had God not promised that He would look to him that is poor and of a contrite spirit (Isa. 66:2)? And are not God's ears open to the cries of the righteous (Ps. 34:15)?

God sees and hears the wicked, however, and this should be a solemn thought for them. Nothing escapes His notice— no sinful deed, no sinful word, no sinful thought. Apart from Christ, God is our judge. Yet, through Jesus Christ, needy sinners like Nehemiah can seek an audience with the great God of heaven.

Think of how Christ displayed His Father's merciful heart when He was on earth. He was so approachable to those who needed Him. His eyes were not closed to the needs of those who came to Him for help, nor was He deaf to those who cried out to Him. Believers can be comforted with the knowledge that they have a High Priest who can be touched with their infirmities (Heb. 4:15).

Confessing Israel's Corruption

At the beginning of his prayer, Nehemiah brings the sins of his people before the Lord. He understood that sin was at the root of their problems. The problem was not their enemies. They were only the instruments that God had used to punish the people for their sins. Their sins had brought about their downfall. So Nehemiah brought those sins to the Lord openly rather than try to hide them.

Notice that Nehemiah confessed the people's sin as his own, using the pronoun "we" (see v. 6). Not only did he use the word "we," but he also even used the word "I." He confessed: "Both I and my father's house have sinned" (v. 6). He knew he was bound in a common sin with the rest of the people, so he did not lift himself above his people or exclude himself from blame.

The reason Nehemiah saw sin for what it was and confessed it so personally was because he had a high view of God. Look again at how he addressed God as the "LORD God of heaven, the *great* and *terrible* God" (v. 5, emphasis added). By "terrible," Nehemiah meant that God should be feared because He is holy and just. When you see something of God's holiness, you will feel your own unworthiness. Even many professing Christians have a view of God that is far too low, and, as a result, a view of themselves that is far too high. By contrast, when Isaiah saw the Lord "high and lifted up," he saw himself as "undone" and "unclean" (6:1, 5).

As he confessed his nation's sins, Nehemiah did not make excuses for or minimize them. He acknowledged: "We have dealt very corruptly against thee, and have not kept the commandments, nor the statutes, nor the judgments, which thou commandedst thy servant Moses" (v. 7). He admitted that they could have and should have known better, for the Lord had given them clear commandments through Moses.

How do we confess our sins to the Lord? Do we try to make our sin appear less than it is? Do we make excuses for our sin or point to mitigating circumstances? When we make light of sin, we make light of Christ's sacrifice for sin. If God could ignore or minimize our sin, why would He have sent His Son to suffer the full penalty of it in His death on the cross and to procure a perfect righteousness?

Pleading Promised Grace

Nehemiah's confession was inextricably linked to his petition. He confessed sin and then sought deliverance from it. Or, you could say, he laid bare the sin, then laid hold of forgiveness for sin.

The essential petition in Nehemiah's prayer was both simple and telling. It boils down to this: Nehemiah asked the Lord to remember His own word that He spoke through Moses (vv. 8–9). In his prayer, Nehemiah pleaded Scripture. He brought God's word back to Him. Undoubtedly he realized that was the only way to obtain God's favor. Nehemiah did not have any ground to stand on in himself or in his people. He had to find it in God, so he prayed: "Remember... the word that thou commandedst thy servant Moses" (v. 8). He is referring here to Leviticus 26:33 and its context, and especially Leviticus 26:42 and 45: "Then will I remember my covenant with Jacob, and also my covenant with Isaac, and also my covenant with Abraham will I remember.... But I will for their sakes remember the covenant of their ancestors, whom I brought forth out of the land of Egypt in the sight of the heathen, that I might be their God: I am the LORD."

Notice that Nehemiah was appealing to the *memory* of God. The Lord had remembered His threat to punish His people. Would He also remember His promise not to destroy them completely (Lev. 26:44)? He wasn't asking for something that had never entered into the mind of God. He didn't suggest some new plan to the Lord. Instead, he asked the Lord to do what He had said He would do: He would *remember* His own promises and oath.

We pray best when we make our petitions on the basis of God's character, or name. That's essentially what Nehemiah did here. God's promises speak of His attributes and portray His power, mercy, grace, and faithfulness. Everything poor sinners need is to be found in God Himself. They need mercy; He is the merciful one. They are helpless of themselves; He has all power. They are unfaithful; He is the faithful one.

Notice, finally, that in prayer Nehemiah brought to the Lord's mind the temple service. He explicitly mentioned the place where God had chosen to "set [His] name" (v. 9). Nehemiah realized that he could best plead on the basis of the Lord's own name. The biblical idea that you would set your name somewhere means that you are putting your character on display in a certain place. Throughout the Old Testament, the place where God set His name on display was the tabernacle and temple (see 1 Kings 8:29), the place where you would find the altar of burnt offering. And, after all, the whole sacrifice system spoke of the way in which sinners can approach a holy and yet merciful God.

In a way, you could say that in prayer Nehemiah was pleading, in advance, the blood of Christ, to whom all the sacrifices pointed. If it were not for Him, there would be no hope. Even the sacrifices could not effect anything apart from what Christ would do in the fullness of time. In Christ there is full redemption for sinful people. Nehemiah understood this by faith, even centuries before the coming of Christ. Now, centuries *after* Christ's coming, do we understand what Nehemiah understood? It is for Christ's sake alone that sinners can be accepted by God and receive help from Him. Christ's work is the perfect pleading ground!

Questions

1. If you had to summarize how God's cause was faring in your church, family, or community, what would you say? Hanani specifically mentioned the walls and gates. Spiritually speaking, how important are the walls and gates to the well-being of a cause?

2. From what we read, Nehemiah went straight to the Lord with His need. How might that convict us?

3. Why is confession of sin always necessary in prayer—not just in times of crisis? Does sin (v. 6) have anything to do with affliction (v. 3)?

4. Why is prayer that appeals to God's character so glorifying to Him and so helpful for our own thinking while we pray?

5. In what way is Nehemiah's prayer in this chapter different from how you pray? What have you learned about prayer from Nehemiah, and how might you pray differently in the future?

6. Nehemiah is concerned to have God's ear attentive to him (see vv. 6, 11). How can we know whether our prayer has reached God's ears?

12

FROM BURDENED TO BOASTING

Nehemiah 2

How can we move beyond anxious questions to confident answers? God's children understand this struggle from the inside out. In Psalm 77, Asaph searched for answers to the questions that plagued him: "Will the Lord cast off for ever? and will he be favourable no more? Is his mercy clean gone for ever? doth his promise fail for evermore? Hath God forgotten to be gracious? hath he in anger shut up his tender mercies?" (vv. 7–9). Just as the Lord gave Asaph renewed confidence in Him, which we see at the end of Psalm 77, so He did for Nehemiah. Nehemiah's first words in the chapter form a doleful question: "Why should not my countenance be sad?" (v. 3). But the last verse in the chapter evidences a very different feeling—a confidence in the Lord: "The God of heaven, he will prosper us" (v. 20). Let's look at how, with God's help, Nehemiah moved from confusion to confidence.

Nehemiah's Sadness for Zion's Ruins

Nehemiah was sad at the king's court. Neither the luxuries nor the festivities that surrounded him could lift his spirits. Although his hands may have held the finest of wines, they were also wiping away the saddest of tears from his eyes. His heart was sinking under a heavy burden. Many people try to forget their problems by surrounding themselves with the fine things of life. But God's children who are sad because of indwelling sin, a sense of being far from God, or home-sickness for heaven find that the things of this world are no comfort to them.

In verse 1, Nehemiah says that he had not been sad in the king's presence before. We know that many kings from this time did not allow those around them to be sad or sul-len; they wanted to surround themselves with good cheer and levity. Don't many in today's world have the same attitude? Their grief, fears, and anxieties about the serious things of life and death are hidden beneath pasted-on smiles and hollow laughs. They pursue possessions, experiences, or rela-tionships, hoping to achieve happiness through them. Many would rather have the crackling of thorns than the rebuke of the wise (Eccl. 7:5–6).

When the king asked Nehemiah the reason for his sad-ness, he answered honestly: "The city, the place of my fathers' sepulchres, lieth waste" (v. 3). Nehemiah was sad about the destruction of Jerusalem. Don't you think this answer would have surprised the king? Why be sad about some distant ruins when you live in a first-class palace?

The world does not know the joys of the Christian, but neither does it understand his sorrows (see Lam. 1:12). Yet, as unlikely as it might seem, true Christians would not want to trade even their sorrows for the world's joys. Artaxerxes can have his cup of wine; Nehemiah will have his cup of affliction if God has given it to him.

Nehemiah's Prayer to Zion's God

Engineers can tell you that large machines often turn on small cylinders. Likewise, God's great providence makes use of seemingly small things; nothing is too small for His use. Let's take a look at the "small" turns of God's providence in Nehemiah 2. God's providence made the king notice Nehemiah's sadness in the first place. Why would a king concern himself with the mood of one of the people in his service? He could easily have ignored or failed to notice Nehemiah's grief. But his eye and mind were providentially focused on his cupbearer. He was led to ask: "Why is thy countenance sad?" (v. 2).

Second, after Nehemiah explained the reason for his sadness, God's wondrous providence again moved the king to ask a follow-up question: "For what dost thou make request?" (v. 4). This was really an amazing question! The powerful king, ruler of the known world, was asking how he could be of assistance to Nehemiah. His military might, financial fortunes, and political position—this simple question placed all of it at Nehemiah's disposal. God's provision for Nehemiah is amazing. Indeed, "how great are thy works! and thy thoughts are very deep" (Ps. 92:5).

Nehemiah did not rush to accept and grab what this rich and powerful earthly king might offer. He first went on an "errand" to heaven, in prayer to God. It was a very quick errand—so quick that Artaxerxes probably didn't even notice. And yet this simple act shows how heavenly minded Nehemiah was. The coals of true devotion were hot in his soul, so little was needed to stoke the fire of prayer. His request jumped like a spark to heaven. In short order, he laid his need before the throne of grace in heaven in order to be able to answer the one who sat on an earthly throne.

Scheduled times for prayer and fellowship with God are essential to a life of true godliness. But God's ears are always open to believers' cries. Through their ever-living high priest, Jesus Christ, and for the sake of His blood, God's children can have constant access to His throne. This may not always be our experience, but it is the truth. And Nehemiah found it to be so at this moment.

Notice that Nehemiah did not possess a spirit of self-reliance and independence. He did not feel that he could answer the king's question without praying about it. Although the king had made him a very generous offer, he did not know how to make use of it without divine guidance. He did not glibly lift his own sails to ride the winds of providence. He wanted to have grace through providence, not providence without grace.

Nehemiah's Forwardness for Zion's Good

Artaxerxes was taking a risk in offering his help to Nehemiah. But Nehemiah was also taking a risk. Jerusalem was just a dot on the empire's map. How did he dare bother the world's most powerful man with the needs of a few nameless pilgrims and strangers on the remote edge of his empire? Perhaps few of us would have dared to make such a forthright appeal. Surely his love for the cause of God motivated him.

Imagine that you worked for a large corporation. Let's say the president of the company asked for suggestions about which charitable causes the company should support. Would the cause of Christ come to your mind? Would you have enough courage to bring up the needs of poor, suffering, and persecuted Christians in places like the Sudan, Eastern Europe, or North Korea? It is amazing how much fund-raising goes on for relatively unimportant causes, like sports teams or animal rights. Have you ever reminded others that although these causes may be good ones, there are many more important causes to support? What about fighting for the rights of the unborn, who in your own city are being killed in their mothers' wombs? Do we try to be a voice for the cause of God?

In essence, Nehemiah asked the king for permission to head up a trip to Jerusalem himself. This was proof of his forwardness and dedication to the cause. After all, he could have asked the king to send someone else to coordinate the work in Jerusalem. He could have stayed safely at the palace in Shushan, among the marbled terraces and golden dishes, while someone else undertook the hazardous trip. But that was not what Nehemiah wanted. He was ready to exchange the comfort and ease of Shushan for the rubble and ashes of needy Jerusalem. He showed a self-sacrificing forwardness to embrace this lowly cause.

Now think of the forwardness of the Lord Jesus Christ, who came in the fullness of time. We are told that it was not robbery for Him to be equal with God (Phil. 2:6). His were the glories of heaven. Yet He was willing to humble Himself unto the deepest reproach and pains of hell both in body and soul. He said with eagerness, "Lo, I come" (Ps. 40:7). Christ's coming to suffer and die for the sins of His people required great humiliation on His part. Like Nehemiah's, Christ's lowliness was for the sake of God's people. So in Nehemiah's concern and forwardness for the people of God, we see a foreshadowing of Christ's sacrificial love and work for sinners. And yet how much deeper did Christ have to stoop!

Nehemiah's Inspection of Zion's Condition

It was clear that the winds of God's providence were in Nehemiah's sails as he entered Jerusalem some weeks later. The king had sent and equipped him on his journey, which had been safe. But Nehemiah didn't rush presumptuously and carelessly ahead once he reached the city. He waited. His waiting didn't mean that he was proud or presumptuous that he knew what to do and how to do it. He waited three days, and then, in the stillness of night, he rose up secretly and inspected the situation on the ground. He held off mentioning to anyone what God had put into his heart to do (v. 12). He went around the city as far as he could. His eyes, which used to see spotless luxury and lavish splendor, now fell upon destruction, decay, and desolation all around him. Things were probably even worse than he had envisioned. Perhaps he knew these words from Psalm 48: "Beautiful for situation, the joy of the whole earth, is mount Zion.... Walk about Zion, and go round about her: tell the towers thereof" (vv. 2, 12). But how different things looked now! Jerusalem's beauty was gone. What would once have been an impressive and awe-inspiring inspection was now a depressing one. But Nehemiah was not turned away from his task. Armed with firsthand knowledge of Jerusalem's wretched condition, he was more prepared for the great work ahead of him.

Think again of Christ's work. In His first thirty years on earth, He moved quietly among fallen humanity, taking in the brokenness all around Him. As the Son of God, He already had a perfect knowledge of our fallen human condition. And yet we are told that, in His human nature, Christ increased in wisdom during His early years on earth (Luke 2:52). He now saw, through human eyes, what sin had done to His creation. It was as if He walked around inspecting the broken gates and ruined walls of a lost world. How this must have impressed on Him the weight of the work the Father had given Him to do!

Nehemiah's Challenge to Zion's Inhabitants

Two of the words Nehemiah used when he talked to the people especially describe Jerusalem's condition: "distress" and "reproach" (v. 17). The word translated as "distress" is actually the word "badness" in the original. "Badness," you could say, is the corruption of goodness, and this is what Nehemiah recognized. He didn't present a plan for progress to the people without first emphasizing the gravity of the situation. "Ye see," he said, "the distress that we are in" (v. 17). Notice Nehemiah's use of the word "we." He included himself, placing himself among the people in their sad situation. Having lived in these conditions for so long, the people of Jerusalem may have gotten used to the "badness" of their situation. But now that Nehemiah had seen it, he specifically reminded the people of it. He detailed it for them: "Jerusalem lieth waste.... The gates thereof are burned" (v. 17). There was ruin, wretchedness, and, as a result, reproach. "Reproach" means disgrace. The city of Jerusalem was open to scorn and contempt in its sad condition. And so Nehemiah minced no words about how things stood.

But Nehemiah didn't stop with the bad news. Nehemiah was focused on *rebuilding* Jerusalem. Even his enemies acknowledged that he had come to seek the "welfare" of Jerusalem (v. 10). For the word translated "welfare," the original Hebrew uses literally the word "goodness." Nehemiah's goal was to make the bad good! And so he challenged the people: "Come, and let us build up the wall of Jerusalem, that we be no more a reproach" (v. 17).

Nehemiah didn't depend on his own strength for this task. He comforted the people by declaring to them the good hand of God (v. 18). He met the *badness* of the people's situation with the *goodness* of the Lord's disposition. There was no use in the people's relying on their own or Nehemiah's goodness. It is only God's goodness that can empower weak hands and raise up distressed spirits. And, indeed, this is what happened: "So they strengthened their hands for this *good* work" (v. 18, emphasis added).

Nehemiah's Confidence in the Face of Zion's Enemies

Nehemiah's confidence in the Lord did not prevent the enemy's attacks; in fact, it increased them. It is not coincidence that when the people committed to the work of the wall, the enmity of their enemies increased. In this case, the enmity was in the form of scornful laughter (v. 19).

This chapter began by telling us of Nehemiah's sadness; now we are told of the enemies' laughter. Heaven works godly sorrow; this unbelieving laughter fits with hell. Yet God sees both, and the time is coming when both will end. God will wipe away all tears from His children's eyes, but

He will also turn all scornful laughter into eternal weeping and gnashing of teeth.

In the meantime, the enemies' taunts should provide opportunities for confident confession, as we see here with Nehemiah. He boasted in God: "The God of heaven, he will prosper us" (v. 20). What had brought Nehemiah from being burdened earlier in the chapter to boasting in God? It was his Godward focus—his faith. In the tenor of Hebrews 11, we could say that by faith, Nehemiah, choosing the reproach of the people of God rather than the riches of Shushan, built the walls of Jerusalem in spite of the taunts of God's enemies. By God's grace and in His time, faith's exercise in the lives of God's people will bring them from being burdened to boasting in God.

Questions

1. What other reasons for sadness do Christians have, other than those mentioned in this chapter? Why can't the world's "wine" help them in their sadness?

2. What can we learn from Nehemiah's spontaneous prayer in the king's court (v. 4)? We know he had been praying for four months (1:1; 2:1). Why would he pray now?

3. Have you known someone who has been very forward about his or her love for Christ and His cause? Doesn't it often seem like the world is more forward about its commitments than Christians are about theirs? Think of ways Christians could change that.

4. Imagine Nehemiah's nighttime tour of inspection. Make such a tour of the Christian church today.

What do you see? Do you ever take a tour of the condition of your own heart? What have you found?

5. Nehemiah's challenge to the people in 2:17–18 was a *courageous* one. What other adjectives would you use to describe it? Explain.

6. How did Nehemiah rise above the laughter of his enemies? What can we learn from this about how to live in this world?

13

SUBMITTING TO GOD'S YOKE

Nehemiah 3

When Christ was on earth, He spoke this invitation: "Take my yoke upon you, and learn of me" (Matt. 11:29). With these words Christ was calling weary ones to submit to His gracious gospel. Submission, however, does not come naturally to us fallen sinners. Unless grace changes our hearts, we resist bowing before the Lord and submitting to Him. We are like bullocks that are unaccustomed to the yoke (Jer. 31:18). When grace intervenes in our lives, we are made submissive to God's call and Christ's yoke, and we begin, in principle, to live for Him.

In Nehemiah 3, we read of many Jews who were building different sections of the wall of Jerusalem. They were motivated by a love for God's service. However, we also read of nobles who were not submissive to this work, who "put not their necks to the work of their LORD" (v. 5). As a result, they missed the blessing of doing what gives most satisfaction in life—seeking God's glory.

The Work of the Lord

In this chapter, the work of the Lord focuses on rebuilding broken city walls. More than a century earlier, in judgment, the Lord had broken down the walls of Jerusalem. He had done so by sending Babylon to destroy the city. The walls that had once signified the strength of God's cause and His presence among His people were in ruins (Ps. 48:12–14). The stones were scattered, and the gates had been burned with fire. The prophet Jeremiah lamented: "The Lord hath cast off his altar, he hath abhorred his sanctuary, he hath given up into the hand of the enemy the walls of her palaces" (Lam. 2:7). Nehemiah, too, had lamented these broken-down walls, as we saw in the first chapter of his book.

Things were about to change. The walls would be rebuilt, brick by brick and stone by stone. Centuries before, God had said through Isaiah concerning Zion: "Thy walls are continually before me" (49:16). Jerusalem was dear to His heart, and He was not going to leave it a desolate place. It was His gracious plan that these walls would be rebuilt. Now, that plan was unfolding.

Our passage emphasizes that the rebuilding was *God's* work. Nehemiah 3:5 calls it "the work of their LORD," confirming what Nehemiah had said earlier: "The God of heaven, he will prosper us; therefore we his servants will arise and build" (2:20). Thus, more was happening than met the eye. The people building this wall were not working on their own. They were servants, doing their Master's work. The Jews could have said along with the psalmist: "This is the LORD's doing; it is marvellous in our eyes" (118:23). Isn't it amazing that the Lord uses frail and feeble human beings as His instruments? And yet the design, purpose, foundation, materials, and strength—everything is His.

Shouldering the Work of the Lord

If someone were watching what the various members of your congregation did all week, would a summary of what he witnessed read something like Nehemiah 3? "Minister X and the elders and deacons rose up and shouldered the work of the Lord in one area. Family A did this part of the work of the Lord; Family B did that part of the work; Family C did yet another part. The people from this ministry group pooled their resources for the project they've undertaken," and so forth. When we read Nehemiah's account in this chapter, this is the picture we get. Each person was doing his or her part. No one was too important for the work, and no one was too insignificant to have a role in the project. Each individual was working toward the same outcome, with the same desire. All were working as one.

Isn't this how things should happen in God's work? Aren't we to see the church of God as a cooperative body? Romans 12:4–6 teaches us: "For as we have many members in one body, and all members have not the same office: so we, being many, are one body in Christ, and every one members one of another. Having then gifts differing according to the grace that is given to us, whether prophecy, let us prophesy." Paul further explains in 1 Corinthians 3:9–10: "For we are laborers together with God.... According to the grace of God which is given unto me, as a wise masterbuilder, I have laid the foundation, and another buildeth thereon." We see from these verses that the work of the church should be very much like the work described in this chapter.

What lessons can we learn from this chapter about how the church is to undertake the Lord's work today?

1. *Those in leadership should show the way.* The high priest and other priests did not refuse to roll up their sleeves, thinking that they were above the work. Instead, they led the way and set the tone (see v. 1). We see here that church leaders are not given their positions in order that they may lord it over others. Rather, like good generals, it is their duty to be the first ones on the battlefield and the last ones to leave it.

2. *We should work together in an orderly way.* We do not read that the people argued about which sections they were going to work on. We don't hear of anyone grumbling that his neighbor's section was preferable to his. The sense that we get is that each person merely took his place next to his neighbor, content with his opportunity to contribute to the work. The people's unity implies their understanding that every part of the wall was important. Viewed from this vantage point, there was no task too menial or too humble. Does this same mind-set guide our work as part of the church body? Do we understand that both big tasks and small ones are equally important? Each member's contribution is vital to the growth and sustaining of the church, no matter how insignificant it might seem. Do we value and pursue a unity of purpose?

3. *We should not shy away from difficult work.* The work of building and repairing the wall would have been hard labor. It involved moving stones, lifting beams, setting up doors, and installing locks. But there is no record in this chapter of anyone complaining about the difficulty of the work. Do we understand that the duties to which Christian service calls us may be difficult ones? It is not always easy to work at our daily calling during the day and then to lead a Bible study,

attend a deacons' or elders' meeting, or visit an elderly member of our congregation in the evening. It is not always easy to give up a Saturday to help members of our church who are in need. It is not easy to be confronted in very real ways with the frailty of life as we visit the sick. It is not easy to seek to correct and guide someone who has fallen into sin. But the Lord doesn't promise us only easy tasks. Let us not be surprised, then, when difficult ones come our way.

4. *Families have an important part in the work*. In this chapter we see sections of the wall being assigned to people who lived in a certain geographical area, such as Gibeon or Mizpah (v. 7); to members of a profession, such as the goldsmiths or merchants (v. 32); or to members of a family, such as the sons of Hassenaah (v. 3). Of particular interest is verse 12, which mentions Shallum and his daughters (he probably had no sons), who worked on a section of the wall. We don't know the age of these daughters, but we can assume that some family groups also would have included young people and children. What a unique opportunity they would have had to participate in this historic building project! They too would have done their part. Let's be encouraged by this to involve our whole families in the life of the church.

Refusing to Shoulder the Work of the Lord

We are reminded, however, that even in times of awakening and blessing there are naysayers. In verse 5, which mentions those from Tekoa, we read: "But their nobles put not their necks to the work of their Lord." What an indictment of these noblemen! Their refusal to work has been permanently recorded in this history, to their shame and disgrace. They did not so much as lift a finger to help build the walls. Let's look closely at the way this indictment is worded in verse 5.

First, the wording hints at the privileges that were theirs. The Lord was "their Lord." In other words, they were not strangers but members of the professing people of God. As such, they were the recipients of many blessings and mercies from Him. They were in the Land of Promise; they ate of the fruit of the land. Because they were nobles, they had probably amassed great wealth. Now that the temple was completed, they were enjoying the privileges of institutionalized worship again. And now they had the unique opportunity to be part of the rebuilding project. But in spite of all these privileges, these men had no heart for the work of God.

Second, the wording shows us their pride. They didn't refuse to be involved in the work because of any sort of inability or out of ignorance. We are told that they "put not their necks to the work." Simply put, they would not submit themselves to it. The implication is that they were lifted up with pride, holding their heads high rather than stooping down as submissive servants. Perhaps the riches and power they had as noblemen were part of the reason for this pride. Perhaps they thought, "Let others do this lowly work. We certainly won't stoop to the level of such menial labor. That would be below us. We'll stay in our mansions and let the common people work." Christ later said, "A rich man shall hardly enter into the kingdom of heaven" (Matt. 19:23). Paul agreed: "Not many mighty, not many noble, are called" (1 Cor. 1:26). Let the attitude of these noblemen serve as a warning to us in the West, who live in great affluence compared to the rest of the world.

Third, the text suggests their spiritual poverty. They did not put on the yoke of the Lord. This means that they remained yoked to something else, for every person has some master. They remained captive to their natural corruptions, their pride and lusts. They missed the sweetness and blessing that God's children know. In Psalm 84:10, the psalmist expresses his contentment with a lowly position in God's service: "For a day in thy courts is better than a thousand. I had rather be a doorkeeper in the house of my God, than to dwell in the tents of wickedness." These nobles would also have missed having communion and fellowship with those who were enjoying the service of the Lord, which is described in Psalm 133:1–2: "Behold, how good and how pleasant it is for brethren to dwell together in unity! It is like the precious ointment upon the head, that ran down upon the beard, even Aaron's beard: that went down to the skirts of his garments." But above all, they missed the approval of God, who has inspired this account of their pride.

May this shameful record of the noblemen of Tekoa spur us on to learn from Christ. He is meek and humble of heart, and in His school, our pride is subdued. Then we learn to take His yoke and find rest for our souls. Truly, His "yoke is easy, and [His] burden is light" (Matt. 11:30).

Questions

1. You could say that this is a chapter filled with a listing of names and facts. What purpose do chapters such as this one serve in Scripture? Why shouldn't we just skip over them?

2. The last verse of the previous chapter, Nehemiah 2:20, helps put this chapter into perspective. How does it help us understand chapter 3?

3. Read Ephesians 2:19–22. In that passage, Paul compares the church to a building in which each believer has a part. What practical implications does this have for how the work of the church should be done?

4. William Tyndale, the Bible translator who made a significant contribution to the church during Reformation times, wrote: "Now thou that ministerest in the kitchen and art but a kitchen page…knowest that God put thee in that office…. Now if thou compare deed to deed, there is a difference betwixt washing dishes and preaching the Word of God; but as touching to please God, none at all." Discuss Tyndale's observation. How does it relate to this chapter?

5. Look again at the four lessons under the section titled "Shouldering the Work of the Lord." Which of these stands out to you? Why?

6. What is it that ultimately keeps us from shouldering the work of the Lord? How can we learn to subdue this?

14

THE CRUCIBLE OF CONFLICT

Nehemiah 4

Many great documents in church history have been written in the midst of intense conflict. Martin Luther's Ninety-Five Theses, William Tyndale's English Bible, John Calvin's *Institutes of the Christian Religion*, and John Bunyan's *Pilgrim's Progress* are just a few examples. Why is great progress often made during times of opposition? One thing to remember is that opposition tests the resolve of the godly, strengthening it in the process. By God's grace, believers who experience it can actually become grounded and settled even more firmly in the truth. In this way, God brings greater glory to Himself: "Surely the wrath of man shall praise thee: the remainder of wrath shalt thou restrain" (Ps. 76:10).

A War of Intimidation

We were introduced to the hostility of the surrounding people back in Nehemiah 2:19. Chapter 4 again mentions Sanballat and Tobiah and the war of intimidation they waged against the Jews (vv. 1–3). Sanballat was the governor of Samaria, the province to the north of Judah and Jerusalem. Tobiah was a leading official in the region east of Judah, often referred to as Ammon. Verse 1 tells us that Sanballat mocked the Jews out of anger. Tobiah soon joined in (v. 3). Inwardly, these neighboring leaders were furious that Jerusalem's wall was being raised again.

Take a closer look at Sanballat's five stinging questions in verse 2: "What do these feeble Jews? will they fortify themselves? will they sacrifice? will they make an end in a day? will they revive the stones out of the heaps of the rubbish which are burned?" In other words, he is saying, "Who do these Jews think they are? With their small resources, they won't amount to anything. Do they think they will make any lasting changes?" Tobiah's words are no less belittling. He says mockingly that a small fox would be able to claw away what they are making (see v. 3).

We read of a similar tactic of intimidation in 2 Kings 18, when Rabshakeh came on behalf of the king of Assyria to speak with Hezekiah's men (vv. 29–35). Rather than immediately launching a military assault, Rabshakeh verbally assaulted them, planting seeds of fear, doubt, and weakness in their minds. He hoped to substantially weaken the morale and strength of the people of Judah.

Today, God's enemies often assault His people in the same way. Rather than issuing an all-out assault against us, which we might more easily recognize, Satan tries to intimidate us psychologically and spiritually. This effective weapon is often successful in immobilizing believers. Many of the Lord's servants have been targets of such assaults.

When their mockery did not accomplish what they had hoped it would, Sanballat, Tobiah, and others with them (the Arabians, Ammonites, and Ashdodites) plotted an all-out attack (v. 8). Their laughter may have died down, but their wrath remained. It simply took on a new face. Instead of laughing jeers and pointed fingers, there were now whispered plots and pointed spears. The wrath of man is ingenious—comparable to a seven-headed monster. Unless it is radically mortified (see Col. 3:8), it is capable of quickly changing faces and taking on new forms. Think only of King Saul in the Old Testament (e.g., 1 Sam. 20:30).

The wrath of evil men against the cause of God will continue as long as this world does. How might God's people effectively withstand it? Verse 4 shows us a very effective weapon against Satan's wrath.

The Voice of Prayer

Notice the way verses 4–5 transition, without any introduction, into prayer to the Lord: "Hear, O our God; for we are despised: and turn their reproach upon their own head, and give them for a prey in the land of captivity: and cover not their iniquity, and let not their sin be blotted out from before thee: for they have provoked thee to anger before the builders." It's as if the enemies' hateful words triggered the builders' prayerful words.

You will recall that Nehemiah had confessed that building the wall was the Lord's own work (2:20). The Jews were working on His behalf. Think of an everyday example from the construction business. If a subcontractor ran into difficulty on a project to which he'd been assigned, you would expect him to notify the general contractor, because as a subcontractor, he is responsible to him. In the final analysis, it is the general contractor's project. These Jews had a similar understanding of their work, so they brought this trouble before the Lord. They said, "They have provoked *thee* to anger" (v. 5, emphasis added).

So when the enemies framed their plot, the builders framed their petition: "Nevertheless we made our prayer unto our God" (v. 9). The enemies sought to storm Jerusalem; the builders stormed the throne of grace. Prayer has its own kind of holy violence (see Matt. 11:12). Would to God that the history of our lives would be characterized by this refrain: *Nevertheless, we made our prayer unto our God.* Trials came to us; *nevertheless, we made our prayer unto our God.* Opposition arose; *nevertheless, we made our prayer unto our God.* Disappointment struck; *nevertheless, we made our prayer unto our God.* Wouldn't we be far less affected by the turmoil of life in the world if we more frequently wielded the weapon of prayer?

The Sword and Trowel

In addition to prayer, the builders also prepared to defend the city (vv. 13–14). We are reminded of the saying "pray and work." Each family defended a part of the wall with swords, spears, and bows. Despite the preparations the people made for conflict, however, not one arrow flew. The mere fact that the Jews were ready for battle was enough to discourage their enemies. And so not one spear left the hand of a Jew; not one sword drew blood. The victory was won silently, without a casualty.

What we see here is something like the battle at Jericho, only in a defensive rather than an offensive mode (see Josh. 6). At Jericho, the Israelites did not need to use their swords to *take* the city; here, the people did not need to use their swords to *keep* the city. At Jericho, the walls *fell down* without a shot; now the walls *remained standing* without a shot. God's overruling providence and power won both of these successes.

Nehemiah kept the people focused on the Lord's power and encouraged them: "Our God shall fight for us" (v. 20). We are reminded of an incident in the early history of the Israelite nation, when the people stood at the brink of the Red Sea. How did they escape the Egyptians who were on their heels? Remember what Moses told them: "Stand still, and see the salvation of the LORD" (Ex. 14:13). It was this same God who would now keep the Jews in safety. They would have the privilege of witnessing His almighty power on display.

The Jews could have cast Tobiah's taunt in verse 3 right back at him: "Tobiah, you were wrong. Your foxlike schemes can't as much as tear down one stone from another." We don't read of them doing that. If God was going to fight for them, there was no need for them to be involved in a war of words with the enemy. Let's take a lesson from this.

The church of God needs to be reminded, again and again, that the battle belongs to the Lord. He won the greatest victory of all at the cross of Calvary, and His victory there secures His people's victories as well. We need not be intimidated by the enemy. As we have seen, the wrath of man is an opportunity for God to get glory (Ps. 76:10).

The Sound of the Trumpet

Sometimes people are so busy acting defensively, protecting themselves from something, that they have no time or energy left for acting offensively. But this was not the case with the Jews in this chapter. They *constructed defensively*, and *defended constructively*. Notice verse 17: "Every one with one of his hands wrought in the work, and with the other hand held a weapon." God had given them two hands, and each hand had a task.

The people's eyes were also busy, although their vision would have been limited as they worked on their separate sections of the wall. This meant that they could not see everything that their enemies were doing. And so their ears were also to be busy, listening for the trumpet sound, which would alert them to danger. So we have the picture of fully engaged hands, eyes, and ears. Every part of the body was devoted to the work. Is the true Christian's warfare of faith any different? The whole being must be engaged, as Ephesians 6:13–20 depicts, and where the apostle Paul instructs us to "take unto you the whole armour of God, that ye may be able to withstand in the evil day, and having done all, to stand" (v. 13). Our hands, eyes, and ears—all must be devoted to the fight that is the Christian's life on earth.

Questions

1. Verse 1 gives us a look into Sanballat's heart. What do we find there? Why would he even care what the Jews are doing? Where do you see wrath against God's work today?

2. The prayer of the builders might be seen as somewhat vindictive (v. 5). What are we to think of this in light of the New Testament's command to love our enemies (Matt. 5:44)? For comparison, consult Revelation 6:10.

3. Read Nehemiah 4:10. Show from the text and context how discouragement is understandable, undesirable, and curable.

4. How does the Christian warfare require the whole Christian? See Ephesians 6:13–20.

5. We see a unified body facing the enemy here. What does that mean about division among our ranks today? What place should spiritual leaders have in the fight of faith?

6. There is a call to the people to fight in 4:14, and the promise that God will fight is in 4:20. Is this a contradiction—or something else? Explain your answer.

15

A REDEEMER COMES TO ZION

Nehemiah 5

The church needs more than protection from the adversaries *outside* its walls. It also needs deliverance from the adversaries *within* its walls. We see an example of this in chapter 5 of Nehemiah. The Jews certainly had their enemies outside their walls, but in this chapter we also see trouble inside the walls of Jerusalem. Let's take a closer look at this chapter.

A Great Cry

Chapter 5 opens with an outcry of one group of Jews against another group, their "brethren" (v. 1). In other words, they were not complaining about "outside" enemies, but about oppression within their ranks, within the community of the Jews. Some commentators believe that the events recorded in this chapter took place during a different time period from the events of chapters 4 and 6. They find it hard to believe that something like this could have been going on at the same time that the people were building the wall together. It is a startling example of *disunity* during a time of such national *unity*! We can't be entirely sure, but the text certainly gives the opposite impression. If these events were from a different

time, Nehemiah surely would have indicated that, as he does
elsewhere (see 13:4–7). Notice also that in verse 16 of our
chapter, Nehemiah mentions continuing his work on the
wall in the midst of this trouble.

As they complain, the oppressed Jews emphasized their
common bond with those who were hurting them: "Now
our flesh is as the flesh of our brethren, our children as their
children" (v. 5). What would cause such disunity among
brothers, other than sin? Wasn't this true even of the first
family ever to live on earth? After the entrance of sin into the
world, Cain's killing of his brother, Abel, showed disunity
and brought anguish into his family circle. Still today, many
know the pain and anguish of being in a divided family. Even
in families that once were closely knit together, bitterness
and enmity can fester for years.

It is even more devastating when the true people of God
cannot work with and love one another. Sadly, this situation
arises too often in churches. But when the Spirit, who unites
sinners to Christ, works within us, we come to realize that
brothers and sisters in the spiritual family must dwell in unity
with each other. As Scripture says, "Can two walk together,
except they be agreed?" (Amos 3:3). How can we build the
walls of Zion if we are busy building walls between ourselves?

Notice the emphasis on *bondage* in this text (v. 5). What
was happening here was outright extortion. The rich were
bringing the poor into bondage and even selling their children into slavery (v. 5). Now sin always brings bondage, and
this situation was no exception. In their pursuit of greater
riches, wealthy Jews were bringing their poor brothers into
bondage. The situation was so bad that the poor Jews could

not keep their sons and daughters out of some sort of indentured servitude. They complain: "Neither is it in our power to redeem them" (v. 5). What a miserable condition! These Jews were powerless and in need of someone to act the part of a redeemer.

A Convicting Challenge

When Nehemiah heard what was going on, he was filled with a holy and righteous anger (v. 6) against this sin. After consulting with himself (v. 7), he called a great assembly against the powerful Jews—the nobles and rulers—detailing to them their sin and its heinous character: "Ye exact usury, every one of his brother" (v. 7). He accused them of violating the law of God. "Usury" means that they were collecting illegitimate or excessive interest on loans they were making. God had forbidden His people to exact interest from a fellow Israelite (Ex. 22:25; Lev. 25:36; Deut. 23:19–20).

When Nehemiah confronted these usurers in this assembly, he managed to get his point across rather readily. We read in verse 8 that those whom Nehemiah accused held "their peace, and found nothing to answer." Sensing their sin, they were quickly silenced. Nehemiah's efforts had been successful! Those who had offended were convicted of their sin.

In addition, Nehemiah's words effected a grand restoration (v. 11). He called for them to "restore" what they had illegitimately taken away. Those who had been extorting from their fellow Jews agreed to return the expropriated properties to their rightful owners. They agreed not to take anything more from them (v. 12). In effect, Nehemiah brought about for the oppressed Jews the same thing that the Jubilee and sabbatical laws were intended to do (see Lev. 25 and Deut. 15). It was tantamount to a Jubilee edict, as God had commanded through Moses. With one stroke, he canceled debts, released fields and lands to their original owners, and set captives free. He also led those he had convicted in swearing a solemn oath to fulfill their duty.

Nehemiah had taken on the role of a redeemer. A "redeemer" is someone who frees captives from the grip of those who have enslaved them. The Bible speaks often of redeemers. In fact, the Lord takes this title to Himself throughout Scripture (see, e.g., Pss. 19:14; 78:35; Prov. 23:11; Isa. 48:17). Isaiah prophesied that a Redeemer would one day come to the assembly of Zion (59:20). One of the things this Redeemer would do would be to turn away ungodliness from Jacob (see also Rom. 11:26). Nehemiah was not the great Redeemer of whom Isaiah prophesied, but in the actions of our passage, he did foreshadow Him.

A Courageous Redeemer

Let's look specifically at two ways Nehemiah foreshadowed Christ's work. First of all, doesn't his convicting work mirror what the great Redeemer does? This Redeemer uses the law of Moses to convict and convince sinners of their sin (Rom. 3:19–20). As He does this, He shows sinners their liability under the law. He makes them lose all their objections and excuses. Sinners must come to acknowledge their sin and confess that what they have deserved because of their sin is just (see Ps. 51:4). Often, Christ does this convicting work through the preaching of the Word, when, with His Spirit, He convicts sinners of sin, righteousness, and judgment to come (see John 16:8). This convicting work makes room for Christ's further work in their hearts and lives.

Second, the restoration that Nehemiah brought about also foreshadows Christ's redeeming work. His sacrifice on the cross brings freedom to those who were once slaves to sin. He brings people who were once alienated and estranged from each other into the family of God to be brothers and sisters to one another. He teaches them to love each other and enables them to do it from their hearts (2 Cor. 9:10–12; see also Matt. 25:40). His people are made generous to others of the household of faith (Gal. 6:10).

Nehemiah could not be a perfect redeemer, for he too was a sinner. He could only effect outward changes—and only for a time. Although he did what he could, his "purchasing power," you could say, was limited. But Christ, the perfect Redeemer, kept the law of God perfectly. He accomplished redemption to its fullest extent, having the power of an endless life (Heb. 7:16). Nehemiah redeemed from physical slavery; Christ, from spiritual bondage and death. Nehemiah redeemed by what he said; Christ, with His precious blood. Nehemiah purchased the people's temporal freedom; Christ, an eternal inheritance with the saints in light. How much greater the work of Christ than even this great redemption wrought through the hand of Nehemiah!

A God-Fearing Ruler

After the great assembly, Nehemiah continued to model a life of sacrificial devotedness to the Lord's cause. He did not demand normal taxes and provisions from the people for the support of his extensive administration. Instead, he used his own provisions. He did not hoard his own resources but dispensed them generously. What motivated Nehemiah to be so unselfish and generous? Verse 15 says that he did it "because of the fear of God." In other words, because God had put the fear of His great name into Nehemiah's heart, Nehemiah had more regard for the Lord—His honor, His cause, and His people—than for himself. This way, he became a beautiful example of godliness to the people. And, all the while, he continued in the work on the wall (v. 16).

Nehemiah's generous spirit reminds us of the apostle Paul, who wrote in 2 Corinthians 11:9 that he had kept himself from becoming a financial burden to the Corinthian Christians. Rather, Paul was willing to spend and be spent for the advancement of the gospel cause.

The gospel calls Christians to have the same generous spirit. Think of how Paul challenged Philemon to take Onesimus back graciously, as you can read in the little epistle of Philemon. He wrote to Philemon: "Receive...not now as a servant, but above a servant, a brother beloved" (vv. 15–16). Paul modeled a generous spirit by his willingness to take any debt Onesimus might have owed Philemon upon himself (v. 18). This is what the gospel does when it is applied by the Spirit. Debts are paid and captives are freed. Grace transforms captors into those who have gracious and generous spirits through Christ, the great Redeemer.

Questions

1. Can you think of any reasons Nehemiah might have thought it right to break away from his narrative of the wall-building efforts to detail the problem of this chapter for us?

2. Discuss from this chapter what the world's mind-set is regarding riches. How should Christians view riches?

3. Read Nehemiah 5:6–8 again. How does what Nehemiah did in these verses happen today spiritually?

4. In what way was Nehemiah's action in verse 11 like the Jubilee? See Leviticus 25:13–14, 25–28, 35–36.

5. Read Psalm 72:12–14. Explain the different ways these verses apply both to Nehemiah and Christ.

16

A FEARLESS LEADER

Nehemiah 6

It doesn't take a lot to bring a Christian down, especially if enemies entice, smear, intimidate, and tempt him or her. Insidious designs can make our hearts faint, our minds flutter, and our spirits sink. Many great men and women have been brought down in the end. Despite many attempts to bring Nehemiah down, he was not deterred from completing the wall.

The Enemies' Devices

In Nehemiah 6, we read that the work on the wall of Jerusalem had progressed to a significant point. Although the doors hadn't yet been set on the gates, the wall was finished to the point that "there was no breach left therein" (v. 1). The enemies of the Jews must have realized their window of opportunity for derailing this monumental accomplishment was closing. Before this moment, they had aimed their attacks at the Jews in general. But now, realizing how crucial Nehemiah's leadership was to the rebuilding effort, they focused their attacks on him personally. If they were going to succeed, they would have to eliminate or sidetrack Nehemiah.

This chapter unfolds four distinct schemes against Nehemiah. The first scheme was *distraction*. Nehemiah's enemies invited him to meet them in one of the villages in the plain of Ono. This area was about twenty-seven miles away, near the coast of the Mediterranean Sea (vv. 1–4). They tried this tactic four times, but each time Nehemiah declined to leave Jerusalem.

The second scheme was *insinuation*. Sanballat suggested in an open letter that Nehemiah was planning to revolt against the king in order to take the throne himself (vv. 5–9). Sanballat's attempts to frighten Nehemiah and weaken his work this way did not bring about the desired result. Nehemiah writes: "For they all made us afraid, saying, Their hands shall be weakened from the work…. Now therefore, O God, strengthen my hands" (v. 9).

The third scheme was *intimidation* into committing a moral infraction (vv. 10–13). This time, Sanballat and Tobiah hired a certain prophet named Shemaiah, who wanted to meet with Nehemiah at the temple. By suggesting a meeting there, Shemaiah attempted to trick Nehemiah into entering the temple without a proper warrant. If this scheme had succeeded and Nehemiah had gone into the temple, he would have committed a moral infraction that would have discredited his reputation among his own people.

Nehemiah recognized the temptation in each of these three schemes (see vv. 9 and 14). In each case Sanballat was hoping he could take away Nehemiah's focus from doing God's will. The weapon Sanballat used in each of these cases was *fear*. Fear is, indeed, a great spiritual crippler. The enemies knew it, and Nehemiah discerned the danger well. His record of responding to each of these tactics is astounding and exemplary.

The final scheme is recorded for us in verses 17–19. We read in verse 17 that the nobles of Judah were in alliance with Tobiah. Intermarriages had cemented these alliances (v. 18; see also 13:4, 28). The networks with the surrounding nations who had been such a threat to the wall-building effort had, as it were, spun a subtle but dangerous web around Nehemiah. Because of these alliances, certain of his own people were informants to Tobiah. They spoke well of Tobiah to Nehemiah, and pressured Nehemiah with his interests (see v. 19). This final scheme, we could say, sought to pressure Nehemiah into *compromise*. His adversaries wanted to bring him down from his resolute commitment to his task and devotion to his God.

It would have been no surprise to read this barrage of tactics had finally worn Nehemiah down so that he gave in to his enemies. And yet that is not what happened! The happy surprise is that, after these various crafty assaults, Nehemiah continued to stand firm. What was the secret to his success?

Nehemiah's Graces

The text points to six dispositions of heart, or graces, whereby Nehemiah resisted the temptation to compromise and proved successful in the end.

1. Nehemiah's *resoluteness*: While the enemies sought to distract him, Nehemiah was resolute in executing the duty that God had laid upon him. He answered Sanballat and Geshem this way: "I am doing a great work, so that I cannot come down: why should the work cease, whilst I leave it, and come down to

you?" (v. 3). He understood the importance of this work and was determined to see it through to its end. And so, although he had been willing to leave his work for the king in Shushan in order to come to Jerusalem, he would not now be willing to set aside the divine mandate for his task. He would allow for no diversion and no interruption.

2. Nehemiah's *forthrightness*: While his enemies' attempts were characterized by insinuation, craftiness, and dishonesty, Nehemiah was forthright and honest. Listen to his clear delineation of the truth: "There are no such things done as thou sayest, but thou feignest them out of thine own heart" (v. 8). He wasn't tempted to answer lies with lies or half-truths with half-truths. He was straightforward. Paul met people like Nehemiah's adversaries. He talked about "the sleight of men, and cunning craftiness, whereby they lie in wait to deceive" (Eph. 4:14). In contrast, a true Christian speaks the truth, shining light into the darkness of falsehood. Nehemiah could be so forthright because he knew the innocence of his own conscience. Proverbs reminds us: "He that walketh uprightly walketh surely: but he that perverteth his ways shall be known" (Prov. 10:9).

3. Nehemiah's *perceptiveness*: God had given Nehemiah the gift of discernment. He was able to look beyond the flattery and trickery in the tactics used against him in order to discern the real motives and intents of those who wanted to hurt him. We see examples of this perceptiveness in verse 2: "But they thought to do me mischief," and in verse 12:

"And, lo, I perceived that God had not sent him."
Nehemiah certainly possessed the "sound mind"
of which Paul speaks to Timothy in 2 Timothy
1:7. He was one of those of whom the writer of
Hebrews describes as having "their senses exercised
to discern both good and evil" (5:14).

4. Nehemiah's *prayerfulness*: We noticed before that
   Nehemiah was a man of spontaneous prayer (chapters 1–2). He was one who continued steadfastly in
   prayer and resisted the wiles of the devil with the
   shield of faith (Eph. 6:16). Despite all the graces
   God had given him, he did not presume upon them,
   but prayed for the continual exercise of them. He
   realized his own innate weakness when left to himself, and so he prayed: "Now therefore, O God,
   strengthen my hands" (v. 9). He could have said
   with David: "Mine enemies would daily swallow me
   up: for they be many that fight against me, O thou
   most High. What time I am afraid, I will trust in
   thee" (Ps. 56:2–3).

5. Nehemiah's *scrupulousness*: Like Joseph, Nehemiah would rather suffer than sin. Joseph's words
   could have been Nehemiah's answer to Shemaiah's
   temptation: "How then can I do this great wickedness, and sin against God?" (Gen. 39:9). Nehemiah
   guarded his heart with all diligence so that he
   would not sin against the Lord (see Prov. 4:23).

6. Nehemiah's *separateness*: Finally, while many even
   in Judah did not see the harm in allying themselves
   with the enemy, Nehemiah would not compromise,
   even in the slightest. Isaiah's motto could have been

> his: "Say ye not, A confederacy [or an alliance]....
> Sanctify the LORD of hosts himself; and let him be
> your fear, and let him be your dread" (Isa. 8:12–13).

In all these points, Nehemiah was what he was only by the grace of God. More precisely, he was these things out of Christ, who strengthened him. While He was on earth, Christ was subject to every temptation, trial, and assault like Nehemiah. Yet no one excelled Him in resolve and obedience. When He was on the cross, mocking voices tempted Him to come down. Like Nehemiah, He essentially answered, "I am doing the greatest work; I cannot come down." When He was tempted to throw Himself from the pinnacle of the temple, Christ said to Satan, "Thou shalt not tempt the Lord thy God" (Luke 4:12). When they came to Him with swords and staves, He said, "Should such a one as I flee?" For that reason, in their fearfulness, believers can receive of His resoluteness; in their weakness, they can receive of His prayerfulness; in their sinfulness, they can receive the blessings of His perfect sinlessness.

God's Purposes

Nehemiah's faith was not put to shame. "So the wall was finished...in fifty and two days" (v. 15). Instead of Nehemiah, the enemies and their tactics were put to shame. Nehemiah had been able to perceive their evil intents, and they now were forced to perceive God's intent. We are told in verse 16, "They perceived that this work was wrought of our God." It's no wonder that the enemies "were much cast down in their own eyes" (v. 16). Their designs had been frustrated, while Nehemiah's had flourished.

What happened at the end of the building of the wall is a picture of what will happen at the end of time. The wicked will be forced to acknowledge with eternal shame, "Our plots were all foiled. None of them succeeded. God performed all His decree." Meanwhile, the righteous will rejoice in their God, who frustrates every one of the schemes of His enemies.

Questions

1. Review the schemes used against Nehemiah in chapter 6. How inventive sin can be! Which scheme strikes you as most daunting? Give examples of how Christ was subject to the same tactics.

2. Find all the references to fear in this chapter. Was Nehemiah ever afraid through all this? (See v. 9.) What can we learn about fear and faith? Read Psalm 56 for further lessons.

3. Find the verses that refer to false prophecy. Where are false prophets today, and how must we resist them?

4. Why did Nehemiah's enemies try to get him to compromise? How dangerous is compromise? What is the best defense against compromise?

5. Read Ephesians 5:6–13. How do these verses shed light on both the devices of Nehemiah's enemies and Nehemiah's graces?

17

WE HAVE A STRONG CITY

Nehemiah 7:1–7

Nehemiah had succeeded in rebuilding the walls of the city of Jerusalem, and its gates had been repaired. Now the city stood, auspicious and armed, as a monument of the Lord's enabling, equipping, and preserving grace. However, it was largely empty: "Now the city was large and great: but the people were few therein" (v. 4).

Was Nehemiah's task finished? Had it all been about stones and mortar? No, God is chiefly occupied with receiving the glory He deserves through His people, who live for Him. And so the strong but empty city needed to be filled with people who would glorify God by grace.

A God-Fearing Leadership

Nehemiah's first task was to appoint leaders. He realized that God raises up leaders to guide His people. The principle of godly leadership runs throughout the Scriptures. When God set out to make Abraham a great nation, He called him to lead. He was to "command his children and his household after him" (Gen. 18:19). When God set out to redeem a people from slavery and bring them to Himself, He raised up Moses to lead the people with his rod. When God set forth to bring His people into the land of Canaan, He chose Joshua to lead them. And so God fulfills His purposes through leaders whom He appoints. They are called to serve Him, execute His directives, and lead others to walk in right ways. Simply put, they must fear God. The fear of God is that grace, worked by the Holy Spirit, which brings people to see both God as He is and themselves as they are. When it comes to leadership, the great benefit of the fear of the Lord is that it frees us from the shackles of public opinion, which is fickle and often wrong.

Nehemiah selected trustworthy and especially God-fearing men to positions of leadership (v. 2). He had not rebuilt this city and withstood all these attacks simply to hand over the city to men who lacked the fear of God. The wall had been built in the fear of God; it was to be enjoyed and maintained in the fear of God.

What Nehemiah did then, Christ would do much later. Christ did not build a literal city, but He did purchase a heavenly city. After His work on the cross was accomplished, He appointed God-fearing apostles to rule the church of God. Still today, ministers and elders are leaders appointed by the ascended Christ over His church and people. They are as watchmen on the walls, and they will have to give account for their leadership (Heb. 13:17).

A Careful Vigilance

Nehemiah did not let down his guard after the task of rebuilding the city was completed. Although the city was practically empty, he was careful not to lose any of the ground that he had gained. He knew the enemies of the Jews would take advantage of any breech in vigilance. Years later, this fear would prove warranted. In Nehemiah's absence, astonishingly, Tobiah himself managed to take up residence in one of the storerooms of the temple (see 13:7). And so Nehemiah put his brother Hanani, along with Hananiah the temple ruler, in charge of Jerusalem's security. Each family would protect the part of the wall near their own home.

Human nature is such that we tend to let down our guard after achieving success. We easily grow overconfident, believing that things will continue to go our way. But we need to be careful about thinking too highly of ourselves. Do we really think that our strength is invincible? Do we reckon with the presence and persistence of our spiritual enemies? They will not simply slink away after losing a few skirmishes. Scripture tells us that Satan has "great wrath, because he knoweth that he hath but a short time" (Rev. 12:12). God's people cannot afford to let down their defenses. Any moment of calm may turn out to be a run-up to another conflict. The church should be always preparing for the next assault. This is the kind of vigilance we see in Nehemiah in this chapter.

A Holy City

Nehemiah wanted to see Jerusalem inhabited. Its vacant lots and empty streets were a sad reminder of the continuing exile of God's people. After all, the Babylonian captivity of the church was still going on, in large part. At one time the city of Jerusalem had been crowded with people, and it was a major pilgrimage destination. The temple worship, with its sacrifices, prophets, and priests, had had a prominent place in Jewish life. But because of the unholiness, compromise, and presumption within the walls of that old city, God had brought judgment. The city had been virtually emptied. And now it needed to be inhabited again.

Nehemiah explained that it was God who had put it into his heart to repopulate the city (v. 5). The building of the walls had been God's work, as Nehemiah 3:5 implied. Now, the settling of the city would be God's work as well. God would be in the process from beginning to end, making this city a "holy city" (see Neh. 11:1).

But who would live in Jerusalem? Nehemiah consulted the genealogy that had been drawn up at the time of the first return from exile (see v. 5). This contained a record of the names of all the people who had returned from Babylon to help build the house of the Lord (Ezra 2:1). In choosing to return, these people had shown a willingness to leave the relative ease of life in the Persian world to return to their homeland. They would have exchanged plentiful food supplies in Persia for whatever they could grow on the rugged terrain that surrounded Jerusalem. Like their forefather Abraham, they had heeded God's call to rise up, leave the land in which they were living, and settle in the land the Lord had promised them. There the temple would be rebuilt, and they could raise their families within sight of the worship of God rather than within sight of the temples to false gods in Persia and Babylon. These people had been set apart as a chosen generation, a holy people, called to show forth the praises of Him who had called them (1 Peter 2:9). These people would fill the holy city of God's habitation.

When we come to Nehemiah 11, we will see the process through which Nehemiah would populate the city (vv. 1–2). In between chapters 7 and 11, we will see Nehemiah preparing the people for life in Jerusalem. The people would need to have the Word of God at the center of their life there (Neh. 8). The people would need to be taught to pray with confession of sin (Neh. 9). The people would need to agree to obey God's law, and their lives had to be consecrated (Neh. 10). These chapters will prove how important it was that Jerusalem would be a *holy* city.

We can't be sure if Nehemiah knew the book of Isaiah, but if he did, he would have understood the significance of what we read in Isaiah 26:1–2: "We have a strong city; salvation will God appoint for walls and bulwarks. Open ye the gates, that the righteous nation which keepeth the truth may enter in."

Let's apply what we have learned from this chapter about the city of Jerusalem to the church. The church of God is still to be a holy city. In His death and resurrection, Christ, whom the Bible calls the foundation stone (Eph. 2:20), erected a new city. By His Word and Spirit, He gathers sinners to be His people within that city. He brings captives home and makes them a chosen generation, a holy people. Life in God's church is to be marked by His own holiness reflected in the lives, attitudes, and deeds of His people (see Zech. 14:20–21). As the parable of the great banquet shows us, God's house will be full, not empty, at His return (Luke 14:23).

Questions

1. Many churches in Western countries have emptied in recent years. Why has this happened? Might there be a connection to the judgment of God, as there was in the case of Jerusalem?

2. What is the fear of God? Further discuss why it is so important, especially for leadership in the home, school, church, and world.

3. Sometimes those who truly fear God wonder what difference one God-fearing person can make. Give examples from Scripture, church history, or your own life of how God can use such a man or woman.

4. What place do vigilance and carefulness have in the Christian life? Why do many people neglect, or even criticize, these qualities?

5. Many today are quite content with a brick-and-mortar concept of the church, the attitude that if things look good on the outside, there's not much else to worry about. How does Nehemiah teach us differently?

6. What does it mean that God put something into the heart of Nehemiah (v. 5)? Does God still work like that?

18

A FRESH SINAI

Nehemiah 8

Long before Nehemiah's time, God had ordained the first day of the seventh month to be the Feast of Trumpets (see Lev. 23:24). This feast was to inaugurate the seventh month, a great month of feasts that also included the Great Day of Atonement and the Feast of Tabernacles. The trumpets were to remind the people of how the trumpet had sounded at Mount Sinai, when God had descended and given His law to the people, taking them as His bride (Ex. 19:5, 13–19; 20:18; Ps. 81:3). A trumpet sound had also served as the marching call for the armies of Israel as they traveled through the wilderness.

God's Word is compared to a trumpet elsewhere in the Scriptures (see Ezek. 33:6; Rev. 1:10). The trumpet of God's Word is sounded frequently throughout the world, yet, sadly, most of its inhabitants never take notice. Even in the church, many are spiritually asleep, even as the gospel is preached. However, when God works reformation, He does it through the trumpet of His Word. That trumpet sound pierces ears, awakens souls, and turns God's pilgrim people into a ready army as they travel through this world to the next.

A Pulpit of Wood

A hunger for God's Word is a blessed kind of hunger. Verse 1 of our chapter says that all of Judah gathered together on the first day of the month to ask that the law of Moses be read. This is really an amazing verse. By nature, we delight in earthly, carnal wisdom but have no appetite for the Word of God. The book of Proverbs portrays Wisdom standing at the street corners, calling in vain for fools to give heed (1:20–24). But here in Nehemiah, the people of Jerusalem gathered in the center of the city and requested that Wisdom speak to them! This willingness to hear was a work of God's grace.

Ezra stood on a pulpit (literally, a tower or podium) of wood (v. 4). In everyone's sight, he opened the book, or scroll, of the law and blessed the faithful Lord (v. 6). The people, obviously impressed with the solemnity of the moment and the majesty of the book, showed a spirit of reverence. Flanked by six men on his right and seven on his left, Ezra read from God's law for most of the morning as the people listened attentively (vv. 3–4).

This wasn't just an empty ceremony that few truly understood. The leaders made every effort to help the people understand the book's contents. They explained the law to the people and helped them understand its meaning (v. 8). Like Philip with the Ethiopian eunuch in the New Testament, the teachers in verse 7 sought to guide the people into the mind, matter, and meaning of the Scriptures (see Acts 8:30–35). Unless Ezra and the other priests had taken such diligent care to expound and instruct, the Jews would have profited little from this reading of the law. It would have remained a "closed book" for them.

Still today, any minister in the pulpit should aim for his hearers' understanding of the Word, so that it will bear upon their minds, hearts, and lives. The Puritan William Greenhill said it well: "Some would have the word only read, and that there should be no preaching or expounding of it. It was not the eunuch's reading, but Philip's preaching, that wrought faith in him…. The spices of the Scripture send forth the strongest and sweetest smells when they are bruised and broken; the fire of the sanctuary yields most heat and light when stirred up and blown."

But the "bruising and breaking" of the Word is no mere human work. Rather, the preacher's great hope and prayer should be that the Holy Spirit would be at work, bringing the Word to the inner ear and inscribing it on the tablets of the heart. He is the great guide into all truth (John 16:13).

Oil of Joy

Isaiah 61:3, a messianic promise, tells us that Christ, as God's appointed and anointed servant, would exchange "beauty for ashes, the oil of joy for mourning, the garment of praise for the spirit of heaviness." This is such a comfort for those who mourn with godly sorrow. Nehemiah 8:9 pictures this for us: "For all the people wept, when they heard the words of the law."

What made the people weep in response to the law? Surely they mourned that they and their fathers had transgressed the commandments of a good-doing God. This will become evident when we look at their prayer in Nehemiah 9. They also may have wept because, despite their many provocations, God, in His goodness, had given them His word.

They may have wept because they were not able to give Him the obedience of which He was so worthy. Certainly, there are many reasons for godly sorrow in the Christian life.

Godly sorrow is a necessary part of true conversion (2 Cor. 7:10). People who hear the law of God but do not mourn to some degree because of their sins are not in the right place spiritually. One great thing God does in conversion is to make a sinner see something of his sin against his Creator. Grief over sin does not come naturally from our hearts. It is not a tendency in certain personality types. Instead, it is something worked by God's Spirit. The focus of this godly sorrow is not primarily punishment. Rather, a person who experiences godly sorrow understands the truth that he or she has sinned against God. It is primarily because of sin that believers weep.

However, as important and necessary as godly sorrow is, it is not the end goal. Resting in a sorrow of heart is not a good sign. Nehemiah, Ezra, and the priests encouraged the people in verses 9 and 10: "Mourn not, nor weep…neither be ye sorry; for the joy of the LORD is your strength." In other words, there is a dual emphasis on law *as well as* gospel, sorrow *and* joy.

In Lord's Day 33, the Heidelberg Catechism explains that true conversion does not consist only of sorrow for sin and forsaking sin, but also new life, which results in true joy:

> *Q. 90: What is the quickening of the new man?*
>
> A: It is a sincere joy of heart in God, through Christ, with love and delight to live according to the will of God in all good works.

It's interesting to note that Nehemiah's name means "the LORD shall comfort." He certainly showed an encouraging evangelical spirit as he and the others spoke comfort to the mourning people. Like the people here, Nehemiah had mourned and wept many days (1:4–5) but had experienced the comfort of which his name speaks.

The gospel of God's grace in Jesus Christ is the ultimate message of comfort, as Isaiah says: "Sing, O heavens; and be joyful, O earth; and break forth into singing, O mountains: for the LORD hath comforted his people" (49:13). There is no comforter like the risen Son of God. Through His Spirit, whom the Bible calls the Comforter, Christ comforts His servants in all their tribulations in order that they might comfort others (2 Cor. 1:4). What an encouragement for Christian ministers to gladly pass out the oil of joy in exchange for the spirit of heaviness over sin!

It reminds us of Christ speaking with Mary Magdalene when He asks her, "Woman, why weepest thou?" in John 20:15. He turned her sorrow into joy by giving her true comfort from out of His finished work and new life. It could also be compared to what one of the elders in the book of Revelation said to the apostle John. He wept because no one was worthy to open the scroll of heaven. Nevertheless, the elder told him, "Weep not" (5:5). There was reason for joy because the Lamb has been found worthy to open the scroll.

Festival of Booths

On the second day of their gathering, the leaders again taught the people. It was on this day that, in God's providence, they found in the law a reference to the Feast of Tabernacles

(v. 14). During this seven-day feast, the Israelites left their homes to live in booths constructed from branches. This feast was meant to be a time when the people remembered their history, their being called out of Egypt to wander as pilgrims in the wilderness toward the Promised Land. It was, you could say, a visible reminder of their pilgrim life. Verse 16 of our chapter tells us that the people of Jerusalem then "went forth, and brought them, and made themselves booths." In other words, they reinstituted the Feast of Tabernacles.

How appropriate the timing was for the celebration of this feast! True reformation will make men strangers and pilgrims in this world. In a world filled with lawlessness and vanity, godly sorrow makes a person eager to walk according to all God's commandments. Though the Christian has, at best, only a small beginning of a new obedience, he or she will be *in* the world, but not *of* it. So it had been with Israel at the foot of Mount Horeb (Ex. 32–33) when God sounded the trumpet of His law and confirmed Israel as a separate nation, a group of pilgrims. The reformation of the people this chapter describes was beautifully symbolized by the celebration of this feast.

Questions

1. Look up the passages about the Feast of Trumpets (Lev. 23:24–25; Num. 29:1–6). Though Nehemiah 8 does not mention the literal sounding of a trumpet, where do you see a figurative sounding of the trumpet in this chapter?

2. Why can there be no true reformation apart from the Word of God? Notice how the Levites helped

explain the Word of God. How important is a person's understanding of the truth of God? What can we do to better understand God's truth?

3. What elements of our worship services do you see in 8:1–12? What elements of preaching do you find represented in Ezra's and Nehemiah's actions here?

4. What are the two main aspects of true conversion, and where do we see them in this text? How do both of these continue as abiding elements in the life of the Christian?

5. Why is it important for Christians to view themselves as pilgrims? What place does the Word of God have in the life of a spiritual pilgrim?

6. In what ways are we more privileged than the people in Judah during Ezra's time? In light of the privileges we enjoy, what can we learn from the Jews in this chapter?

19

THE PRAYER OF
RETURNING PRODIGALS

Nehemiah 9

In this chapter, we see the people of God making large strides on the way home. Like the younger son in Christ's parable of the prodigal son, these people are turning back to the One against whom they have sinned. In fact, though this prayer is much longer than the prodigal's speech to his father, the same four elements are present, as we will see.

First, however, we need to set the context. Some days after the Feast of Booths had ended, on the twenty-fourth day of the same month, the Jews gathered for a solemn assembly. They fasted in sackcloth and put dust on their heads as a sign of contrition (v. 1). This was a day of separation from the wicked around them and of confession of their own and their fathers' sins (v. 2). Verse 3 tells us they spent time ("one fourth part of the day") in reading the law, and another fourth part of the day they confessed sin and worshiped. Led by certain Levites, whose names are listed in verses 4 and 5, they then moved into corporate prayer. In this great prayer, a prodigal people return to their God in four steps.

Remembering God's Greatness

When the prodigal in Christ's parable came to himself, he began to remember his father and his father's house (Luke 15:17). He now thought of his life at home very differently from when he left. It's highly meaningful that the prodigal's return involves a significant change in his view of his father, for in true conversion it is an important turning point when we begin to think of God differently from the way we did when we turned our backs on Him.

So, too, the prayer of Nehemiah 9 begins with the people's acknowledgment of God's being, majesty, greatness, and faithfulness: "Thou, even thou, art LORD alone; thou hast made heaven, the heaven of heavens, with all their host, the earth, and all things that are therein, the seas, and all that is therein, and thou preservest them all; and the host of heaven worshippeth thee" (v. 6). In past years, the Jews wandered from this God. They had been lured away to worship the gods of the nations around them and forgot the Lord, who had nurtured them and given them every blessing they had ever received. But now they have to confess that their God is "LORD alone," who has made everything in heaven and earth (v. 6).

In order to be weaned away from the emptiness of false religion, we need to have an accurate picture of who God is. That is such an important starting point! In our day, the church's main problem is that it does not have a functioning doctrine of God—at least not a biblical one! When we begin to realize who God really is, all our religious games come to a quick end, and we begin to realize with whom we are dealing. Dr. Martyn Lloyd-Jones once said, "There is no doubt but

that 99.9 percent of our troubles as Christians is that we are
ignorant of God." The truth that God is a great God calls for
great reformation.

Recalling God's Goodness

Second, the prodigal in Christ's parable not only had thoughts
of his father, but, specifically, he also thought of his father's
goodness even to his servants (Luke 15:17). Paul tells us that
it is the goodness of God that leads to repentance (Rom. 2:4).
The people in Nehemiah 9 also remember past instances of
the Lord's undeserved kindness and faithfulness. He had
remembered His promise and covenant. He had performed
the mercy promised to their forefathers, even though they
had not deserved His mercy. Time after time, even after His
people had wandered from Him and sinned against them,
He had dealt with them in love and faithfulness. The Levites
enumerate the acts of the Lord: "Thou didst divide the sea....
Thou leddest them.... Thou camest down...and spakest...
and gavest...and madest known...and commandedst...and
gavest them bread from heaven for their hunger, and brought-
est forth water...and promisedst them" (vv. 11–15).

This enumeration of the Lord's acts ought to stir up in
us a similar desire to praise Him. How many things, must
we confess, has He done for us—individually, as a nation,
and as a church? Why has He not let the church remain lost
in error? Why has He kept it and prospered its growth, in
spite of persecution? Why has He given revivals, such as the
Reformation and the Great Awakening? Why has He raised
up godly ministers who have preached the truth? Why hasn't
He simply taken away the candlestick of His Word from our

own countries, in spite of our national sins and wayward-
ness? Why are you still not consumed, despite all your sins?
Can the reason lie with you?

Isn't it because to Him belongs the heart of a tender
mercy? Let us confess with the Levites: "Nevertheless for thy
great mercies' sake thou didst not utterly consume [us], nor
forsake [us]; for thou art a gracious and merciful God" (v. 31).
May the truth of God's love in Jesus Christ humble us and
draw us back to Him as prodigals time and time again.

Vindicating God's Justice

In Christ's parable of the prodigal son, the prodigal's words
show us that he understood what he deserved because of
his sin: "I...am no more worthy to be called thy son" (Luke
15:21). He had forfeited his right to be a son, and he acknowledged this honestly and forthrightly before his father. In
Nehemiah 9, we see the same honesty of spirit in the Jews'
prayer. They confessed: "For thou hast done right, but we
have done wickedly" (v. 33). Rather than making excuses for
their sin, or accusing the Lord of unfairness, they *vindicated*
Him while they *incriminated* themselves.

Let's take a moment to apply this lesson to ourselves.
Through our sin we have departed from God's truth and
ordinances. We, too, have sinned away all right of being
received by Him in tender mercy. But so often we live as
though we had a right to all the privileges of God's grace!
A sense of entitlement so easily clouds our understanding of
God's grace, and we spend more time excusing ourselves than
exalting the Lord. We need to join in this prayer of the Jews

and say in all honesty, "Thou art just in all that is brought upon us; for thou hast done right" (v. 33).

If we are still in the far country or in a backslidden condition, we have only ourselves to blame. If God has given us up to our own devices, He has done so justly because of our wickedness. What need we have to come humbly before the Lord and declare, "Thou hast done rightly, for we have acted sinfully."

Pleading God's Grace

The prodigal's return to the father's house included the cry, "Father," or, as Paul would say so memorably, "Abba, Father" (Rom. 8:15). This tender address expressed the prodigal's plea for acceptance in the father's house, even though he knew he did not deserve it. He pleaded with his father, "Make me as one of thy hired servants" (Luke 15:19). The prodigal was begging for a small morsel of grace, only to be allowed to serve his father as master, but he still calls him father (Luke 15:21).

A similar plea came from the people in our chapter: "Now therefore, our God…who keepest covenant and mercy" (v. 32). Notice that the people say "*our* God" (emphasis added). How did they dare to call upon God as *their* God? They knew that there was nothing in them that deserved to have this God as theirs, for they, like the prodigal son, had departed from Him. Away in a far country, they had been as good as dead. But now, having come back into the land, they called out to Him as "our God."

How can sinners, who don't deserve to be called God's children, call God their Father? Only for the sake of Jesus Christ. *He* was the perfect Son of the Father. He did the work His Father had given Him to do perfectly. Through Him, sinners are adopted as sons into the family of God.

Do you feel the need earnestly to beseech the covenant-keeping Lord to remember mercy toward you for His name's sake? Returning to Him, may our petition be like these prodigal people: "Our God…let not all the trouble seem little before thee" (v. 32).

Questions

1. Why is repentance so connected with realizing truly the character of God: His greatness, goodness, justice, and grace?

2. How is the people's exile to the nations whose idols they worshiped a picture of how our sin has led us into bondage? Why does the world promise freedom when it can't deliver on its promise?

3. What does it mean practically to vindicate God? Why is this important? What must we say if a person cannot bring himself to confess the justice of the Lord? How significant is this for our prayers?

4. Find the petition in this nation's prayer (hint: it's somewhere between verses 30–34). Why is it so short? Shouldn't they have prayed for more?

5. Discuss the implications of Dr. Lloyd-Jones's statement: "There is no doubt but that 99.9 percent of our troubles as Christians is that we are ignorant of God."

20

BIBLICAL COVENANTERS

Nehemiah 10

The prophet Jeremiah looked ahead to the day when God's people would return, weeping and seeking the Lord, with these words: "Come, and let us join ourselves to the LORD in a perpetual covenant that shall not be forgotten" (Jer. 50:5). In Nehemiah 9, we saw the first part unfolding: Israel *weeping* over their sins. Now, in chapter 10, we see the second part: God's people *joining* themselves to the Lord in *covenant* with Him.

Covenanting is not a familiar concept in all branches of the Christian church. However, it was a common concept among the Puritans and those who followed them. To "covenant" means to formally commit to certain duties or responsibilities by pledge or promise. A good example is the covenant a man and woman make in marriage.

The Bible mentions covenants often. Although they were at times made between two individuals, they were usually undertaken by God Himself. For example, we read in Scripture about God establishing His covenant with individuals like Noah, Abraham, and David (Gen. 6:18; 17:7; Ps. 89:3). In the time of Moses, God established His covenant with the nation of Israel, constituting them as His people (see Ex. 20:1–21). All of these covenants that God undertook, you could say, are offshoots of the great covenant of grace, in which God committed Himself to the salvation of sinners through the blood of His Son, Jesus Christ. It is this covenant that undergirds the whole gospel as it is unfolded in Scripture.

When we consider our response to the covenant, we need to be careful that we don't view people as being on the same level as God. Those who are in covenant with the Lord are not the initiators but the *receivers of* and *responders to* God's covenant of grace. They are not bargaining with God or seeking to earn salvation through works. Instead, they are wholly accepting and embracing the covenant obligations He has required of them. Paul called his readers to live in covenant with God in response to the gospel of free grace through Jesus Christ: "I beseech you therefore, brethren, by the mercies of God, that ye present your bodies a living sacrifice" (Rom. 12:1).

This is exactly what these people are doing in our chapter. In repentance and faith, they are responding to God's call and gospel. They have come to see that they cannot live apart from the Lord. They need to be devoted to Him by His grace. He is worthy of their all, so, together, they will put their names to the covenant that He had undertaken from His side to draw them to Himself.

Though we see a whole people covenanting with the Lord here, covenanting has taken place on various levels. For example, the well-known National Covenant (1638) and Solemn League and Covenant (1643) were made at the national level in Scotland. Covenanting takes place on a family level when a whole family turns from a life devoted to sin and the world to serve the living God. They join an existing gathering of the people of God through expression of covenant promises, or vows. Covenanting can be done on an individual level; Joseph Alleine, Jonathan Edwards, David Brainerd, and Ebenezer Erskine were all men who expressly formulated resolutions before God.

The Covenanters

Chapter 10 is the climax of what has been happening in the previous chapters. It never just happens that people bind themselves to the Lord in covenant. In chapter 8, Ezra and the leaders read the law and explained it to the people. In chapter 9, the people had responded with confession of sin and prayer. Now, in this chapter, we see them responding to the law in an even more concrete way as they sign their names to a covenant with the Lord. What had begun with the powerful preaching of God's Word by Ezra and the others issues into a public commitment to the Lord.

This covenant was not something entered into only at the general group level. Those who signed the covenant made a personal, public, and permanent commitment to abide by it. The list of many who signed in verses 1–27 shows us Nehemiah's emphasis on individual accountability to it. Nehemiah uses the word "sealed" to describe this public commitment (v. 1; see also 9:38). We don't know exactly what this sealing involved, but the implication is that the covenant became an official legal document, just as a marriage certificate; once it is signed, it is sealed by a county clerk or other government official and becomes a legal document.

Notice that Nehemiah's name heads the list of signers. The names of the priests follow in verses 1–8 (among whom is Seraiah, probably Ezra's full name), then the Levites in verses 9–13. Verses 14–27 list the names of the "chiefs of the people." Finally, verse 28 tells us that the rest of the people signed, "having knowledge, and having understanding" of what was involved in their commitment.

We don't know much else about the thousands of people who added their names to this covenant. We know almost nothing of their stories, social rankings, individual lives, or families. We don't know what happened to them after the events of this chapter. But we do know that they were wholly taken up with this covenant. They were now covenanters in the sense that identities had become linked to this covenant. They would not be known so much as rich or poor, learned or unlearned, masters or servants—but by their relationship to this solemn covenant.

The Covenanting

What was the substance of this covenant? The chapter tells us two main things. First, it involved separation from the people around them (v. 28). Second, it involved a vow to follow God's precepts (v. 29).

It is clear that this separation was both *from* something and *to* something. If you think about it, this would be true of every covenant. We cannot enter one allegiance without leaving another. We cannot bind ourselves to someone without leaving behind others. The Puritan Joseph Caryl, in encouraging his audience to enter into covenant with the Lord, wrote: "Every man must look to it, that he takes this covenant with a heart emptied of all covenants which are inconsistent with this…. Every man by nature is a covenanter with hell, and with every sin he is at agreement: be sure you revoke and cancel that covenant, before you subscribe this." Thus, the Jews in this chapter separated *from* the people of the surrounding nations and separated "*unto* the law of God" (v. 28).

Of course, separation from the world would not be necessary if we were not fallen sinners. We would already be in communion with God, in a right relationship with Him. However, as Paul writes, we are all by nature walking according to the course of this world (Eph. 2:1–3). The course of this world has its own rules and regulations, which are in opposition to God's laws. Many people do not see the dichotomy between God's laws and the world's laws. They live as if it were possible to get the best of both systems. But that can't happen. The underlying foundations of this world's systems are totally in opposition to the gospel of Jesus Christ. There can be no partnership between light and darkness, life and death, Christ and Satan.

We need grace to separate us from this world. We must understand, though, that our separateness is not to be merely external. If we have merely an outward separation from the world, unaccompanied by an inward *heart* separation, we are still falling short. We are reminded of the Israelites wandering in the wilderness. Although they had been physically freed from bondage in Egypt, most of them were still allied to the principles of Egypt in their affections. This kept them in spiritual bondage and darkness. We need God to take hold of us and separate our affections and wills from their unholy alliance with sin and darkness. *Then* we will be free to live in holiness and righteousness as it is found in Jesus Christ alone. Only *then* will we begin to experience what it means to be separated unto the Lord.

Like the Jews' leaders, who were the first to stand up and embrace this covenant, fathers and mothers must lead their families in living whole lives of separation from the world. As families, we must aim at holy and consistent lives of separation unto God, dependent on His grace. May God revive among us a sense of the need to live according to God's statutes and commandments!

The Covenant

What, specifically, did these covenanters promise to do? They did not invent a new code of ethics, new traditions, or a list of behaviors they deemed fitting. Rather, they promised to abide by the ancient Word of God, specifically as it had been delivered by Moses (v. 29). They weren't concerned about man-made laws, but rather commandments, statutes, and precepts God handed down to them through Moses that were preserved in the Word of God.

The ordinances to which the people agreed are specifically listed in verses 30–39. Many of these ordinances, as we noted, stood in opposition to the lifestyle of the surrounding nations. God's people were particularly to avoid intermarriage, keep the Sabbath, and maintain the worship of God. These three categories of ordinances relate back to what God instituted at creation. Time and again, the world has launched assaults at these three basic institutions, and we see this today with the attack on the institution of marriage, the trampling underfoot of the Sabbath, and the neglect of God's name and cause. Instead of living according to God's institutions, people live for their own pleasure, convenience, and self-service.

When God brings His people into covenant with Himself, He brings them under the sway of His own reign and rule. And when people, by grace, come under God and submit themselves to Him, to obey His Word in His strength, they are fulfilling the reason for which God created them. People cannot, of course, do this of themselves. We need to be engrafted into Christ. That way Christ's perfect obedience to God's Word will be ours. His redemption from sin and transgression will also be ours. Have you learned to look away from yourself and bring all your covenant-breaking back to the Lord, confessing your sin? At the head of Nehemiah 10 stands Nehemiah. But at the head of the eternal covenant stands Jesus Christ, who could truly say, "I delight to do thy will, O my God: yea, thy law is within my heart" (Ps. 40:8). Let us seek from Him and His Spirit the grace of covenant fulfillment.

Questions

1. How would you explain the beauty of what the people in this chapter did to those who think it all sounds legalistic and works-oriented?

2. What characteristics of good leadership do you see in this chapter? What role should heads of households serve in leading their families to live in obedience to the Word of God?

3. What is the importance of knowledge? (See v. 28.) There is a lot of *information* out there, but what disciplines are needed to foster good *knowledge*?

4. Why do *separation from* and *separation to* go hand in hand? Is it possible for people to *separate from*, but not *separate to* something?

5. It's interesting how important the creation ordinances are in this chapter (Sabbath, marriage, worship). How is Satan attacking these three things today? How does this chapter instruct us to respond?

6. How are baptism and confession of faith instances of covenanting? Is there any place for personal or group covenanting today? If so, give an example.

21

THE HOLY CITY

Nehemiah 11

Chapter 11 is largely made up of names of people who made Jerusalem their home. At a quick glance, it might seem there is little to learn from this chapter, but a closer look shows differently. The focus of the chapter is the *grace that gathers* people into the walls of the holy city to live in the shadow of God's appointed means of grace. Those who lived within these walls enjoyed the precious privilege of living close to where God had appointed the true worship of His name.

Initially after the walls were built, it seemed like few were eager to live in Jerusalem. Back in Nehemiah 7 we saw that the city remained largely empty. In our contemporary world, this might strike us as strange. Today, large cities attract many people because of the opportunities and excitement they offer. But that was not the case with Jerusalem at this point in history. There were all sorts of reasons many people would naturally have preferred not to live there. Let's take a closer look, then, at how Jerusalem became filled with people.

Overcoming Reluctance

At the beginning of chapter 11, we read that the leaders of the people lived in Jerusalem. However, verse 1 mentions that the rest of the people cast lots to bring one out of every ten remaining people to live in the city, while the remaining nine would live in other towns. Why hadn't the Jews voluntarily decided to move into Jerusalem? This chapter does not tell us why casting lots might have become necessary, but we can guess a few of the reasons that moving into Jerusalem wasn't an ideal option for many people. First, the people who lived in the city would be moving into a danger zone of sorts. After all, the city had been the target of hostility. Memories of the recent planned attacks by Sanballat, Tobiah, and others were undoubtedly fresh in the Jews' minds. Perhaps many of them thought that Jerusalem was a relatively unsafe place for their families.

Second, the economic system at this time was land based. As we saw in Nehemiah 5, life was not easy in this kind of system. Poor growing conditions due to unfavorable weather and taxes could seriously reduce profits. But leaving the land behind to live in Jerusalem would not have made things any easier. Even if a person kept the farm on his inherited land operational, managed by hired workers or relatives, things would be more difficult to oversee. Life in a newly rebuilt city was uncertain, and only time would tell if the city would succeed. If city dwellers ever needed to leave the city to return to their land, would it be profitable enough to provide for their needs?

A third deterrent may have been that Jerusalem was called the "holy" city (see vv. 1, 18). Considering our sinful natures, we shouldn't be surprised that some of the Jews might have had misgivings about living in a city that was known as a consecrated place. Who is eager to take on a standard of holiness that goes above and beyond that to which others are holding? Think, for example, of the Sabbath day. There were watchmen, gatekeepers, priests, Levites, and rulers in Jerusalem; this would mean more accountability and more pressure to conform to strict Sabbath-keeping. But in the countryside, with more distance between people and more privacy, people would be freer to live as they liked on the Sabbath without others noticing their activities or holding them accountable. These factors may have increased people's hesitation to move to Jerusalem.

Experiencing Renewal

The events of chapters 8–10, however, may have helped people think differently about living in Jerusalem. Through the reading of the law and the preaching of Ezra and the Levites, the Lord had renewed the people. He had brought them under the claims of His Holy Word and testimony (chapter 8). This had showed itself in the people's heartfelt prayer of confession (chapter 9) and many people's commitment to the covenant (chapter 10). God's people were experiencing a divinely worked awakening in their minds and hearts. If God had not been working in His people in this way, Nehemiah would likely have had more difficulty persuading them to move into the city.

There is an application for us here. God alone can change the heart! A desire for holiness and a readiness to submit our will to God's are things that only He can give. We can do nothing in our own power to cultivate them. Therefore, we ought to pray for God to give, and then strengthen, a love for holiness among us. We need our reluctance to holiness overcome by the holy God Himself.

Exhibiting Readiness

Verse 2 of our chapter mentions those "that willingly offered themselves to dwell at Jerusalem." The wording here implies that when the lot had fallen upon this 10 percent of the population, they showed a willingness and readiness to pack their belongings and move to the city. We do not get a sense of coercion but rather of willing compliance with the outcome of the lot. God's Word had evidently done its work of mollifying the people's hearts. They had learned to come under the covenant and submit their interests to God's cause. Although earlier they may have resisted the move, perhaps now they recognized the privileges that would be theirs as inhabitants of the city.

What would those privileges be? First, to dwell in Jerusalem meant to dwell where God had chosen to dwell (Ps. 132:13). The people had been reminded that their life was nothing more than a pilgrimage (8:13–18), which their dwelling in booths signified. And under Ezra and his preaching, God had worked a renewal that had inflamed the people's hearts to love holiness. Living in Jerusalem, in the presence of God, would remind people of their heavenly habitation and their love of holiness.

Second, the temple service was prominent in Jerusalem. Living so close to the altar of burnt offering, the people would have had the privilege of being visually reminded of the precious redemption God was foreshadowing in the sacrifices. What an object lesson for those who had been redeemed out of bondage! This was no doubt one of the reasons it was so appealing for the priests, Levites, Nethinim, and singers to come within the walls of the Lord's holy city. They could have echoed what the psalmist recorded in Psalm 84: "For a day in thy courts is better than a thousand. I had rather be a doorkeeper in the house of my God, than to dwell in the tents of wickedness" (v. 10).

Third, the city of Jerusalem was a city of praise and worship. Chapters 11 and 12 repeatedly speak of singing and worshiping. The city walls would have often been filled with the praises of God's people, with songs of redemption, mercy, and grace. As Psalm 46:4 reminds us, Jerusalem is a joyful city: "There is a river, the streams whereof shall make glad the city of God, the holy place of the tabernacles of the most High." The people who lived in the city would have the frequent experience of the Lord inhabiting the praises of His people (see Ps. 22:3).

God is the source of our true submission and sacrifice to Him. Scripture tells us that He makes people "willing in the day of [His] power, in the beauties of holiness" (Ps. 110:3). Today, we often consider it a hardship to bend our schedules around the worship of God. Many have no trouble moving far away from faithful houses of worship for earthly advantages. The grace of God must change us to see how suitable and lovely the cross is compared to everything that this world offers. Because we deserve by nature to be banished from God, it is a miracle that God has provided a holy city and called people to dwell close to Him. It is another miracle when He gives us the all-consuming desire to be planted in the house of the Lord (Ps. 92:13).

John Newton knew this well. By His grace, God drew this wandering, rebellious sinner to Himself. Newton wrote about his experience in the hymn "Glorious Things of Thee Are Spoken," using these fitting words:

> Savior, since of Zion's city
> I through grace a member am,
> Let the world deride or pity,
> I will glory in Thy name.
>
> Fading are the worldling's pleasures,
> All their boasted pomp and show;
> Solid joys and lasting treasures
> None but Zion's children know.

Questions

1. What did the renewal in Nehemiah 8–10 have to do with the events of chapter 11? (See 7:4.)

2. According to Nehemiah 11:2, the people blessed those who willingly offered themselves to live in Jerusalem. In the church today, what situations might produce this same thankfulness and wonder in us?

3. When the people cast lots (v. 1), it was as if providence laid upon certain ones the burden of answering this call. We don't usually draw lots; still, divine providence has other ways of calling people into service. How do we learn to willingly and not reluctantly offer ourselves in such instances, and how do we know for sure this is what God has in store for us?

4. Verse 2 emphasizes that people were willing, not forced, to live in Jerusalem. How does God make men willing to follow His call, whatever it is?

5. What can you find out about Perez (v. 6) from Genesis 38:25–29, in light of the whole chapter, and Matthew 1:3? (He is also called Pharez and Phares.) Why is it amazing and encouraging to read of so many of his descendants among the inhabitants of Zion? What lesson does this contain for today?

6. Verse 22 shows that God desires singers in His holy city so that they would lift up their voices in song to Him. Study a few passages on singing and its importance in serving the Lord (Ps. 22:3; Col. 3:16). How might singing have a greater place in your family and personal life?

22

LOOKING BACK IN WONDER

Nehemiah 12

God created mankind to praise and glorify Him. It is in praising and glorifying Him, then, that we find our greatest fulfillment and purpose. One important gift from God is singing, which is mentioned often in the Bible. The first reference to it comes after Israel's deliverance from Egypt (Ex. 15:1). There, on the banks of the Red Sea, Moses and the people sang a song of praise to God. Revelation 15:3 records the Bible's last reference to singing. There, on the sea of glass, the redeemed sing the song of Moses and the Lamb to praise God for His final deliverance from sin and the devil.

Nehemiah 12 mentions "singing," "singers," and "songs" nine times. It mentions "thanks" or "thanksgiving" seven times, and another seven times we find related words such as "joy," "gladness," and "rejoicing." Verse 43 describes the scene beautifully: "Also that day they offered great sacrifices, and rejoiced: for God had made them rejoice with great joy: the wives also and the children rejoiced: so that the joy of Jerusalem was heard even afar off." You could say that the events of this chapter are a fulfillment of Psalm 87:7, which says of Zion: "As well the singers as the players on instruments shall be there." The Jerusalem of Nehemiah's day was not the perfect New Jerusalem, but it is a picture of how, even on earth, the Lord puts a new song into His people's hearts (Ps. 40:3), which will continue to resound through all eternity.

A New Generation

The first part of chapter 12 continues the lists and genealogies from verses 20–36 of the previous chapter. In this part of the list, the focus is on the priests and Levites, including the Levites who specialized in singing. Verses 1–9 give us the list of priests and Levites who returned home with the first generation of immigrants. Verses 10–26 give us the names of their descendants. Though this detailed list of names may seem uninteresting, it does serve a number of purposes.

1. *It shows that this whole record is all history.* The book of Nehemiah is not just a vision for reform. It isn't just an inspiring story. If it were, these details would be useless. Instead, these events actually took place! These details give validity to this historical account.

2. *It shows that God's work continues.* These verses show us the continuation of the priestly line. As one generation passed away, another generation took its place. God raised up new men to serve Him, along the lines of families. Sons followed their fathers, assumed their offices, and sought the furthering of God's cause.

3. *It shows that God uses a variety of gifts and persons in His cause.* It would have been understandable if we had been given a list of the governors and perhaps also the high priests. However, the list goes beyond

this. It includes helpers to the priests—namely, gatekeepers who guarded storerooms (v. 25) and others responsible for praise and thanksgiving (v. 24). As Paul says elsewhere, God's cause is not furthered only through leaders, but by every member of the body; there are "diversities of gifts, but the same Spirit" (1 Cor. 12:4).

What a blessing it is when God raises up a new generation to serve Him! There has been so much apostasy, especially in the West, in the last few centuries. Even in our own day, sadly, there are so many young people who do not see the value and beautiful privilege of serving the God of their parents. We need to pray that God would raise up and equip a new generation that is faithful to the God of their fathers.

A Finished Fortification

This chapter not only celebrates God's faithfulness through the generations, but it also celebrates the completion of the walls (vv. 27–43). A dedication of the walls ceremonially marked the end of Nehemiah's building project. The desire of his heart had been fulfilled!

Of course, the walls were not an end in themselves. They were meant to encircle and protect Jerusalem so that the city would be "a praise in the earth" (see Isa. 62:7). This is what Jerusalem had been when Solomon first built it. Over time, however, its worship had become formalistic and even corrupted. You have only to turn to the prophecies of Isaiah and Jeremiah to find out how things in Jerusalem had deteriorated. As a result, God had ultimately given this city up to its enemies. He had removed His glory from the temple and city, and, consequently, the Babylonians destroyed both.

Jeremiah had lamented the defilement and destruction of Jerusalem (see Lam. 1). The exiles had hung their harps on the willows and refused to sing the Lord's song in a strange land. Now that God's favor had returned to His people and Jerusalem was once again built up, wasn't there reason to pick up their instruments and praise Him?

A Holy Celebration

Verses 27–43 give us a wonderful picture of how the dedication of the walled city unfolded. There were three main elements to this dedication.

1. *Consecration.* The Hebrew verb translated as "dedication" in verse 27 is *hanukkah*, later used as a name for the Jewish feast that commemorates the rededication of the temple (see John 10:22). The verb could also be translated "consecration." The word literally means "to inaugurate" and especially applies to altars, the temple, and other things used in worship. In this case, the wall itself was consecrated to God's service.

2. *Purification.* The priests and the Levites first purified themselves, the people, the gates, and the wall (v. 30). Notice that even the wall needed purifying! What a testimony to the defiling character of sin. Of course, external washings and sprinklings by earthly priests could provide only a picture of purification. True purification is only through Jesus Christ. The epistle to the Hebrews pictures such purification as the purging of the conscience from dead works to

serve the living God (9:14). The same passage tells us that Christ purified the "things in the heavens" with His own blood (9:23). This is somewhat difficult to understand, because nothing in heaven is defiled and in need of purification. However, this verse likely means that Christ applied His blood *even* to the place where He would receive His people, in order that all communion with God, both in heaven and earth, would be through His one sacrifice.

3. *Celebration.* The dedication included loud and joyful celebration. Two groups marched in parallel formation on top of the walls until they met at the Fish Gate. Each of these groups was led by a thanksgiving choir (vv. 31, 38), followed by lay leaders (vv. 32, 38, 40), then seven priests with trumpets (vv. 33–35, 41–42), and finally a chief musician and group of singers (vv. 35–36, 41–42). This was not just pomp and circumstance. It was an expression of joyful hearts. The people as a whole, including women and children, joined in praise. There was such joy and rejoicing that the text calls it "the joy of Jerusalem." It is noteworthy that this joy was not self-produced, but *God given.* We read: "God had made them rejoice with great joy" (v. 43).

We should pause and remember how Nehemiah felt back in the first chapter of this book. Then, he was weeping because of the sad state of God's people, land, and worship. Now, near the close of the book, Nehemiah's weeping has been turned into joyful worship. How significant it is that the same city, over whose ruins he once mourned, is now a source of great joy for him. He could have echoed David in Psalm

30:11: "Thou hast turned for me my mourning into dancing: thou hast put off my sackcloth, and girded me with gladness."

Questions

1. Several psalms bring together the concepts of Zion and joy (or singing). See, for example, Psalms 48, 87, and 132. Why do these concepts fit so well together?

2. The culture around us displays a lot of shallow joy. On the other side, there are people who emphasize somberness over joy for the Christian. What is true joy, and what does it mean to "rejoice with trembling" (Ps. 2:11)?

3. People today talk about "worship wars"—disagreements congregations can have about how to worship God. Why do you think there were no worship wars in this passage? Look at verse 46.

4. Sometimes people claim that the frequent references to instruments in the Old Testament give us warrant to use instruments in worship. But there are other elements of Old Testament worship (such as priests, Levites, purification rituals, and offerings) that we don't use today. What does the New Testament emphasize when it refers to singing? Consult Ephesians 5:19–21 and Colossians 3:16.

5. Verses 44–47 of this chapter tell us what arrangements were made to continue the service of God. Here we learn that the people loved their ministers and "rejoiced for the priests and for the Levites that waited" (v. 44). In the same spirit, what are some things we could do for our ministers?

23

CLEANSED!

Nehemiah 13

There is a subtlety to sin. It covers its tracks, blinds the eyes of the sinner, and often moves him or her, even imperceptibly, into further sin and evil. This is true on a personal level, but it is also true corporately. Churches, families, and institutions can all be led astray by the subtlety of sin. For example, what many in a church think of as spiritual progress might actually be spiritual regress. It takes someone whose eyes have been opened by God's grace to understand the evil of evil, expose it, expel it, and exchange it with good. Nehemiah had been given extraordinary grace for this, as we see in this last chapter of his book.

The Temple Defiled and Cleansed

In verses 4–14 of this chapter, we learn that while Nehemiah was away from Jerusalem for some time, earlier reforms had been reversed. Allowed to go unchecked, sin had festered. Very important institutions had been corrupted—the temple was defiled, the Sabbath was desecrated, and marriage was dishonored. These were blessings God had given for the people's good, but they had been misused.

So God sent His servant Nehemiah, once again, to shine the light of His Word on the people's sins. In this light, these sins would appear as they really were—exceedingly sinful (compare Rom. 7:13). Nehemiah also ordered and undertook the cleansing of these beautiful institutions. We should see Nehemiah here as a type of Jesus Christ, who cleansed His people from all their sins and consecrated them to God. His is a far more extensive cleansing than anything Nehemiah was able to do in this chapter.

One of the most shocking things we read in this chapter is that Tobiah, an unrepentant enemy who had tried to stop the rebuilding of Jerusalem, now had a foothold in the city—and not just in the city, but even in the temple! Verses 4 and 5 tell us that Eliashib the priest had prepared a room for him there. Imagine Nehemiah returning to Jerusalem after some time in Shushan only to find, as it were, Tobiah's name on the door of a room in the temple! God had specifically instructed that "an Ammonite or Moabite shall not enter into the congregation of the LORD" (Deut. 23:3), and now Tobiah had office space in the very courts of God! Verse 5 calls the space he was using a "great chamber," which was the room where tithes for the Levites and other temple servants had been stored.

How had this sad development come about? You could say that it happened because Eliashib, the one who was to guard the temple, had not guarded his heart. That is where the problem began. Verse 4 explicitly says that Eliashib "was allied unto Tobiah."

Thankfully, Nehemiah recognized this development as evil (v. 7). We should thank God for men who are able to discern what is evil and who aren't afraid to call it what it is! Discernment like this is a work of God's grace. Our natural hearts are not sensitized to sin. One of Satan's goals is to blind our eyes and hearts so that we do not recognize evil for what it is. Sometimes, this happens over time. What once seemed sinful may, as time passes, look less threatening. Later we may think of it as only something neutral, and, if our blindness continues, we may even come to the point where we "call evil good, and good evil" (Isa. 5:20).

Nehemiah, however, was sensitized to sin. It grieved him. This is what true godly sorrow works in the heart. According to Paul, godly sorrow shows itself in, among other things, "carefulness," "indignation," "vehement desire," and "revenge" (2 Cor. 7:11). This is exactly what we see in Nehemiah's reaction to sin. With a holy boldness, he "cast forth all the household stuff [of] Tobiah out of the chamber" (v. 8). He showed something of the zeal that we see later in the Savior, who was consumed with zeal for the house of the Lord (John 2:17). Like Christ, who overturned the tables of the moneychangers (John 2:15), Nehemiah commanded that the chambers be cleansed and the rooms restored to their proper use—namely, the storage of tithes. He also set up a committee of faithful men to oversee the proper collection and distribution of the tithes (v. 13).

Though Nehemiah cleansed the temple in a substantial way, he could not do what Christ alone can do. Christ not only cleansed the outer courts of the temple, but He also cleanses the inner sanctuary of sinful hearts. When He does this, He makes all things new. He also gives His people the Holy Spirit as a wise and faithful leader and guide.

The Sabbath Desecrated and Sanctified

Next, in verses 15–22, we read that Nehemiah noticed that the Sabbath was being desecrated. Some Jews were working their crops on the Sabbath; others were buying from merchants of Tyre on the Sabbath. Nehemiah was not afraid to confront those who were not keeping the Lord's Day. He even spoke out against the authorities, who had turned a blind eye to this sin. He asked: "What evil thing is this that ye do, and profane the sabbath day?" (v. 17). These nobles may have thought that since they were not the ones breaking the Sabbath, they were free of guilt. As those in positions of leadership, however, they were part of the problem. Because they were *omitting* to do what they were supposed to do, others were *committing* what they were not supposed to do. What a responsibility it is to be a leader in the household of faith—or even a leader in the home! Not speaking out against sin that happens on our watch makes us guilty of it—a sobering thought.

Nehemiah showed himself to be a courageous and godly leader by challenging other leaders to rule righteously and set the example. He even took an extra step to beat sin back. According to verse 21, he confronted the merchants from Tyre, who had set up camp outside the city gates. Presumably, they were planning to enter the city when the opportunity arose. Nehemiah saw what a threat this was to the Jews' keeping of the Sabbath. Sin lay crouching at the door (see Gen. 4:7), and it needed to be curtailed. Nehemiah's response shows how concerned he was to nip sin in the bud.

Nehemiah did not just act negatively, in the sense of forbidding certain activities on the Sabbath. He also took positive action. He instructed the Levites to cleanse themselves so that they could aid the people in sanctifying the Sabbath day (v. 22). What a delight the Sabbath can be when we use it as God has ordained! Sadly, we often don't know what is best for us. We regularly let the world encroach on the day of rest that God has given us. How we should seek the cleansing of Christ's blood and the new obedience that can be found in the Lord of the Sabbath Himself!

Marriage Dishonored and Reformed

In verses 23–31 of this chapter, we see how Nehemiah dealt with the Jews who had misused God's gift of marriage. There are many ways in which we can misuse this institution. Many people rush into marriage without thinking carefully about the consequences of their choices. Others don't invest in their marriage as they should, withholding their love, energy, and time from their spouse. So often, too, we do not appreciate our spouse as we should, nor do we see what a blessing God has given us in marriage. In this chapter, the Jews were abusing the institution of marriage by entering into mixed marriages with people of the surrounding nations.

Verse 23 tells us that Nehemiah saw Jews who "had married wives of Ashdod, of Ammon, and of Moab." As we saw earlier in Ezra, mixed marriages were a real temptation for the Jewish people. They often married people from surrounding cultures who had not wholeheartedly joined the people of God. Today, mixed marriages remain a problem. A plague in the household of faith, they often bring grief and pain into the marriages and cause problems for the church. The children of these mixed marriages also suffer as a result of their parents' choices. Verse 24 tells us that the children of these mixed marriages "spake half in the speech of Ashdod, and could not speak in the Jews' language, but according to the language of each people."

Why would someone enter into a mixed marriage? Sadly, many people quickly become careless, especially when their emotions get involved. Sin has the tendency to hide or excuse itself. How we need discretion, discernment, and submission to God's Word! How parents need both wisdom to give biblical guidance to their children in this area and also courage to face a teenage son or young adult daughter when they come home with a modern-day "Ammonite."

We can tell from what he said to the people that Nehemiah knew the power and authority of the Word of God. He used the example of Solomon, who had been led away by heathen women, to convict the people of their treacherous actions (v. 26). In one particular case, he even dared to chase away a priest who had married into the family of Sanballat, the Jews' enemy (v. 28).

When the rest of the world or the church commits and countenances sin, courageous leaders like Nehemiah search it out and stand against it. We should thank God for godly leaders. There still are people like Nehemiah who stand up for what is God-honoring, despite what others say or do. In the power of Christ, let us seek to emulate his godly example. See in Nehemiah the faint outline of Jesus Christ, who gave Himself for the church, "that he might sanctify and cleanse it with the washing of water by the word, that he might present it to himself a glorious church, not having spot, or wrinkle, or any such thing; but that it should be holy and without blemish" (Eph. 5:26–27).

Questions

1. How was Nehemiah aware of the subtlety of sin and the damage it does? Find and read the references he makes to evil in chapter 13.

2. How can leaders be guilty of the sins they don't personally commit? What does this say to us if we are church officers, parents, or in some other position of leadership?

3. How did Nehemiah use the Word of God in verse 26? What can we learn from him about its importance in the battle against sin?

4. What are some of the ways that Nehemiah nipped sin in the bud in this chapter? Why do you think this is important? Give examples of how we can do this.

5. Some think that Nehemiah's prayers sound self-righteous. Look carefully at verses 14, 22, and 31. What does he express his need for?

LESSONS FOR MINISTRY FROM EZRA

Though he lived in Old Testament times, Ezra speaks in many ways to the life of a minister today. Descending from a priestly line, he was most notably a scribe in the laws of Moses (7:6). He came on the scene about seventy years after the first return from exile. We are told that he "prepared his heart to seek the law of the LORD, and to do it, and to teach in Israel statutes and judgments" (7:10). Clearly, like the man in Psalm 1:2, his delight was in the law of the Lord.

You could call Ezra 7:10 his personal mission statement. He was characterized by an unquenchable thirst for three things: (1) to know God through His Word, (2) to walk the way of His Word, and (3) to be used to bring others on this way of God's Word. All three of these things by themselves are a weighty calling—and how much more all three of them together!

What Ezra was pursuing in all of this was true Word-based, Spirit-worked reformation. It is true that Ezra did not use the word "reformation." In fact, Scripture uses that word only once, in Hebrews 9:10, where the writer speaks of the setting aside of ceremonies and Mosaic ordinances because

the fullness in Christ had come. Ezra used a more picturesque term, which gets at the essence of what reformation is
all about. Ezra used the term "to beautify" the house of God
(7:27). The picture is that of a building that needs renovation
and beautification. But the focus of Ezra's ministry was not a
physical building. What Ezra wanted most was that the people of God would appear clothed in the beauty that His Word
gives them through the powerful operation of His Spirit.
John Calvin said it well: "Christ adorns the Church His bride
with holiness as a pledge of His good-will.... The true beauty
of the Church consists in this conjugal chastity, that is holiness and innocence."[1] This is the driving motivation of every
true reform movement in the history of the church of Christ.
In essence, this is the calling of every minister.

Ezra's ministry unfolds in two segments, one of which
is narrated for us in Ezra 7–10 and one in Nehemiah 8–10.
These two segments correspond with a dual emphasis in
Ezra's ministry. The first shows how Ezra engaged in a *convicting* ministry (Ezra 9–10); the second, how he fostered an
equipping ministry (Nehemiah 8–10). Let's look more closely
at each of these in turn.

A Convicting Ministry

A convicting ministry like Ezra's will be marked by a number
of things. First, it *uncovers a compromising spirit*. Compromise, by definition, involves concession. When the spirit of
compromise enters the realm of biblical truth and results in

---

1. John Calvin, *Commentaries on the Epistles of Paul to the Galatians
and Ephesians*, trans. W. Pringle (repr., Grand Rapids: Baker, 1999), 321.

weakened principles, it is devastating. When we form a compromise between a biblical principle and an unbiblical one, we lose the biblical truth.

Ezra's ministry showed that the Word of God must be brought to bear on the reality of sin. If the Word does its work under God's hand, sin will appear as sin. Paul said it well when he was reflecting on his own experience of conviction: "For I was alive without the law once: but when the commandment came, sin revived, and I died" (Rom. 7:9).

Second, a convicting ministry produces a *humble* spirit. By our nature, we make much of people—their abilities, their positions, their approval or disapproval, and their standards. But conviction does the opposite. It puts sinful nature in its proper place. To humble ourselves before God means to abase ourselves before a good-doing God, claiming no rights, making no excuses, and arguing no mitigating circumstances. We approach Him only with sin, shame, and guilt. Ezra demonstrated this humble spirit in 9:15: "We are before thee in our trespasses: for we cannot stand before thee because of this." Self-abasement involves confession of sins in their specificity and depth.

Third, a convicting ministry yields a *God-glorifying* spirit. Many people mistakenly think Ezra was overly strict and legalistic. They imagine that the New Testament presents a radically different message from the one Ezra was sending. However, Paul's words to the Corinthians were as sharp as Ezra's:

> And what concord hath Christ with Belial? or what part hath he that believeth with an infidel? And what agreement hath the temple of God with idols? for ye are the temple of the living God; as God hath said, I will dwell in

them, and walk in them; and I will be their God, and they shall be my people. Wherefore come out from among them, and be ye separate, saith the Lord, and touch not the unclean thing; and I will receive you, and will be a Father unto you, and ye shall be my sons and daughters, saith the Lord Almighty (2 Cor. 6:15–18).

When the people in Ezra's day took upon themselves the work of separating from the nations around them, they were essentially doing what Paul later commanded: "Be not conformed to this world: but be ye transformed by the renewing of your mind" (Rom. 12:2). This certainly brings glory to God, for He has made us for Himself, and we have been made for His honor.

An Equipping Ministry

There is always a wonderful balance within Scripture between law and gospel, sin and grace, sorrow and joy. Likewise, in Ezra's ministry we see a progression from conviction to edification, from breaking down to building up, from pruning to planting. This is the focus of Ezra's ministry according to Nehemiah 8–10. There were few men in the Old Testament who had a ministry so focused on equipping the people of God.

We could define an equipping ministry as follows: *An equipping ministry focuses on furnishing God's people with the necessary tools for practical, sanctified living before God.* Or, to say it another way, an equipping ministry seeks to outfit God's people with all the necessary knowledge, encouragement, and prompting to live as kings and priests in this world in worship, holiness, and witness to the glory of the Triune God.

How is this accomplished? First, an equipping minister *aims to reach the minds of his hearers.* Ezra and his associates exposited the content of the Word of God and applied its truths to the people (Neh. 8:7–8). He was clearly convinced that the Word had to reach the people's minds. There should be no doubt about its content and relevance to each person. Ezra was convinced that if this people were to be reformed at all, it would have to be by the Word addressing their minds. Nehemiah 8:8 explains: "So they read in the book in the law of God distinctly, and gave the sense, and caused them to understand the reading." The Princeton theologian Archibald Alexander echoed this same truth: "By a clear exhibition of Gospel truth, on all the important points of religion, the people should be so instructed, and so imbued with the truth, that error shall make no impression on them."[2]

Second, an equipping ministry *seeks to direct the heart.* Ezra counseled the people in their response to the Word. The text tells us that they lamented (Neh. 8:9). By the operation of the Holy Spirit, these truths that Ezra had aimed at their minds had such an effect that the people could not help but react with great mourning. They were lamenting their sins and were impressed under the judgments of the Lord, as they are announced in the books of Moses. This is clearly a very natural response to the work of the law as it is brought home to the conscience. But note how Ezra sought to guide the people's response. Together with the others, he counseled them and sought to direct their response. We

---

2. Archibald Alexander, "Rightly Dividing the Word of Truth," in *The Princeton Pulpit*, ed. John T. Duffield (New York: Scribner, 1852), 34.

read in Nehemiah 8:9–10: "This day is holy unto the LORD your God; mourn not, nor weep.... Go your way, eat the fat, and drink the sweet, and send portions unto them for whom nothing is prepared: for this day is holy unto our LORD: neither be ye sorry; for the joy of the LORD is your strength."

We see here how pastorally focused Ezra was as he took the people by the hand and led them further. Instead of a cold objectivism, we see here a rich and full emphasis on the subjective experience of faith. He showed a sympathizing or priestly ministry that gave spiritual guidance to needy people. He showed them how the people should direct their hearts and in what direction they should move.

The Puritans are well known for exactly this—guiding the hearts and responses of their hearers. They were often called soul-physicians.[3] This is in keeping with Proverbs 13:17: "a faithful ambassador is health." They counseled people on their response to the Word and sought to direct them further: from sadness to joy, from questions to answers, from doubt to assurance, from affliction to hope.

Third, an equipping ministry is eminently *practical*. It targets our devotion to God, giving it real hands and feet. Think of the covenanting ceremony in which Ezra led the people to pledge before God to live their lives devoted to Him. The covenant addressed such things as marriage, worship, and giving. The climactic line of the whole covenant ceremony was, "and we will not forsake the house of our God" (Neh. 10:39). Ezra's equipping ministry reoriented them very

---

3. J. I. Packer, *A Quest for Godliness: The Puritan Vision of the Christian Life* (Wheaton, Ill.: Crossway, 1990), 43.

decidedly and practically around the house of God. The people would now live in a way that revolved around the service of the Lord.

A ministry that addresses only the mind will end up in objectivism and rationalism. A ministry that addresses only the heart will promote subjectivism and mysticism. A ministry that activates only the hands will result in activism and pragmatism. A ministry that addresses the whole person will, under the blessing of the Spirit, equip the body of Christ in her duty and calling.

It is not difficult to see in Ezra's equipping ministry the shadow of the Mediator's unparalleled ministry. Ezra read the word as a prophet, ministered to the grief of the people as a priest, and directed the people's actions as a king. But therein he foreshadowed that great Scribe—or Secretary—who not only proclaimed the Word but also was the Word; not only counseled the Word but also lived the Word; not only acted in accord with the Word but also inscribed the Word on the heart by the power of His Spirit. Christ and His Spirit are the great hope to make the church truly attractive. Her beauty appears at the behest of and through the gracious work of her beautiful Bridegroom. Ultimately, Ezra's ministry fulfilled God's promise: "For the Lord taketh pleasure in his people: he will beautify the meek with salvation" (Ps. 149:4).

May God grant us days of reformation again, furthered by convicting and equipping ministries like Ezra's,

> till we all come in the unity of the faith, and of the knowledge of the Son of God, unto a perfect man, unto the measure of the stature of the fulness of Christ...

from whom the whole body fitly joined together and compacted by that which every joint supplieth, according to the effectual working in the measure of every part, maketh increase of the body unto the edifying of itself in love (Eph. 4:13–16).

~ Appendix 2 ~

LESSONS FOR PRAYER FROM NEHEMIAH

Christ tells us that the "violent" take the kingdom of heaven by force (Matt. 11:12). He was saying that the kingdom does not belong to those who are willing to go along only half-heartedly. In every age, those who wrestle with the Lord at the throne of grace will accomplish spiritual good in and around them with His help.

The book that bears his name shows Nehemiah to be a man who used much spiritual violence to advance the Lord's cause in his time. Think of how he built Zion's walls by storming heaven's gates (1:4). He opened Persia's purse by taking hold of heaven's King (2:4). He staved off Zion's enemies by calling on heaven's Captain (4:4). He reformed Zion's people by making them swear an oath not to exact interest from their fellow Jews (5:12).

One of the frequent ways Nehemiah exercised this spiritual violence was in prayer. You could compare him to a spiritual lion, like Elijah, who shut off heaven's dew and then brought it down again through effectual, fervent prayer. Spurgeon pictured this type well: "The Christian zealot… prays like a man who means it. He comes up to heaven's gate, grasps the knocker, and knocks, and knocks, and knocks again, until the door is opened. He gets hold of the gates of heaven, and labors to shake them to and fro as though he would pull them up, bolts and bars and all, as Samson did the gates of Gaza, rather than not prevail with God."[1] Such was Nehemiah.

Let's take a look at Nehemiah's prayer life in order to learn how we might be such "violent" people today, with the help of the Lord.

1. *Have a great view of God.* Nehemiah's preferred title for God is the "God of heaven" (1:5; 2:4, 20). This shows the high regard he had for God. God is in the heavens; He has at His disposal the hosts of heaven, and everything on the earth is at His command. He is the great God, the terrible God, enthroned in majesty and state. He speaks but a word, and judgments come on the earth. He has but to remember His word of promise, and the course of history is altered. When we realize the greatness of God in our prayers, we will be compelled to seek great things of God.

2. *Have a low view of yourself.* Indissolubly related to a high view of God is a low estimate of one's own abilities, state, and powers. Nehemiah's preferred term for himself is "servant" (1:11). He knew his weakness and prayed for strength (6:9). He knew his need for great mercy and prayed accordingly (13:22). He knew himself bound up with his people, sharing

---

1. Charles Spurgeon, "Zealots: A Sermon Delivered on Sunday Morning, July 16, 1865," in *The Metropolitan Tabernacle Pulpit* (repr., Pasadena: Pilgrim, 1979), 391.

their faults and their sinful nature, and thus confessed their sins as his own (1:6). If we have a low view of ourselves, we will make recourse to the Lord in prayer our first action, not our last. Knowing our great helplessness drives us again and again to the great helping God.

3. *Have a deep sense of spiritual need.* By light from on high, Nehemiah understood the depths of the Jews' troubling condition. He did not think lightly of it. He didn't just think the best of it all and imagine that it would correct itself in time. When he heard about the walls and gates of Jerusalem, he realized that the city of God was vulnerable to attack. It was not prospering; God's name was not being honored in Zion's low estate. Neither did he see his rank or ability as a match for the deeply spiritual problem. This need drove him to fervent prayer. The Puritan Samuel Rutherford once said, "Dry wells send us to the fountain."[2] When we perceive our spiritual state, apart from God's grace, to be dried, shriveled, and parched, how can we not run, as thirsty people, to the fountain of living water?

4. *Have a great burden for the cause of God.* Nehemiah did not pray for his own good only. He was deeply moved by the condition of God's people at that time. He was profoundly taken up with God's promises for restoration. The honor of God drove him. The low condition of Zion in his time furnished him with much impetus and earnestness in prayer. Our hearts must be knit to the heart of Christ, and

---

2. Samuel Rutherford, *Letters of the Rev. Samuel Rutherford*, rev. and ed. Thomas Smith (Edinburgh: Oliphant, 1891), 216.

when they are, the burden that Christ has for God's people becomes our burden. We must cultivate a holy love for the things Christ cherishes.

5. *Consider the biblical help that fasting can provide.* One of the first indicators of Nehemiah's fervency in prayer is the posture he details: "I sat down and wept, and mourned certain days, and fasted, and prayed before the God of heaven" (1:4). External things like fasting can never be a substitute for prayer, but there is much biblical instruction on the practice of fasting, especially in the New Testament (Matt. 6:16–18; Acts 14:23). Of course, merely depriving our bodies will do nothing for us spiritually. If we are participating in a ceremony or even performing a work just to make ourselves acceptable to God, it can never profit us. When we fast in dependence on God, according to His Word, it helps enliven the soul to feed on God and His Word.

6. *Maintain in dependence on the Spirit a frame of continual prayer.* One of the most obvious characteristics of Nehemiah's prayer life was its regularity, spontaneity, and constancy. For Nehemiah, prayer was like a live fire that needed to be stoked, fed, and kept ablaze. A life of continual prayer is never easy, especially for our sinful flesh, which is the epitome of self-sufficiency. Yet to depend on God to instruct and help us in prayer is key. Nehemiah prayed in season and out of season so that the path to the throne would never be overgrown with brush. He labored to have fresh and regular access to his Master above. For us, too, prayer must be our very breath. Nehemiah shows us that prayers do not need to be long, verbose, or public. It is the God-centeredness by

which we pray that makes our prayers effective for the sake of Christ.

7. *Make trials triggers for prayer.* Nehemiah was in the habit of seeing his difficulties as calls to prayer (4:4; 6:9; 13:29). The enemy's assaults could gain no advantage over him because every assault would trigger a prayer. The more the enemy assaulted him, the more Nehemiah prayed to God. He was like a sentry on an outpost in the battle; if the enemy moved to attack, Nehemiah sent a message up to his Captain for divine reinforcements. If every attack and trial Providence sent our way drove us to prayer, the enemy's designs would be greatly confounded. As Elijah called down fire upon the enemies of God, we must call down the fire of God against all that would spiritually hinder our holiness and God's glory.

8. *Keep short accounts with God.* When we harbor sin in our hearts, the spirit of prayer wanes. When David kept guilty silence, his strength dried up. When he confessed transgression, God heard and answered (Ps. 32:5). The psalmist stated, "If I regard iniquity in my heart, the Lord will not hear me" (66:18). Throughout his memoirs, Nehemiah readily acknowledged his corruption (1:7), and he continued in guarding his heart and confessing his sin (9:33). We know what it is like to allow issues to fester and grow. Being quick to repent and seek the face of the Lord will not only prove to be for our good, but it will also further show the continual need for prayer.

9. *Always rest on mercy.* Some have thought that Nehemiah leaned on his own works. They refer to Nehemiah 5:19:

"Think upon me, my God, for good, according to all that I have done for this people." This is, however, a misunderstanding. He was not pleading his own righteousness as a ground of acceptance before God. He was praying for God's thoughts to be turned to him for good. He desired that his work for his people would not fall to the ground. It is in the same vein as Moses's prayer: "Establish thou the work of our hands" (Ps. 90:17). Nehemiah rested on mercy until the very end. One of Nehemiah's last recorded prayers was, "Spare me according to the greatness of thy mercy" (13:22).

10. *Live a dedicated and dependent life.* When we live out of love for the Lord and His cause, we can draw strength from the fact that what we desire and long for (if it is right) is not something the Lord is reluctant to grant, but rather is most pleased to grant. Nehemiah radiates this confidence of faith: "The God of heaven, he will prosper us; therefore we his servants will arise and build" (2:20). Dependence cultivates prayer, and prayer cultivates dependence. The more we pray, the more dependent we become. And the more dependent we realize we are, the more we pray. In many regards, prayer is the single, most humbling discipline God commands of us—because it is the embodiment of dependence.

Matthew Henry once wrote: "When God designs mercy, he stirs up prayer."[3] Who can tell? If we would pray like Nehemiah, perhaps we would see merciful days like his.

---

3. Matthew Henry, *Commentary on the Whole Bible* (repr., New York: Fleming H. Revell, n.d.), 1:419.